SHOCKING
STORIES
—OF THE—
CLEVELAND
MOB

SHOCKING
STORIES
—OF THE—
CLEVELAND
MOB

TED SCHWARZ

THE
History
PRESS

Published by The History Press
Charleston, SC 29403
www.historypress.net

Front and back covers: Courtesy of Cleveland State University Cleveland Press Collection
and Cleveland Public Library Photograph Collection.

First published 2010
Second printing 2013

Manufactured in the United States

ISBN 978.1.59629.918.4

Library of Congress Cataloging-in-Publication Data

Schwarz, Ted, 1945-
Shocking stories of the Cleveland mob / Ted Schwarz.
p. cm.
ISBN 978-1-59629-918-4
1. Organized crime--Ohio--Cleveland--History. 2. Mafia--Ohio--Cleveland--History. I.
Title.
HV6452.O3S39 2010
3641..1'060977132--dc22
2010039765

CONTENTS

PART 1
EVERYBODY LOVED THE STATLER

Discovering the love affair between the mob and Cleveland's Statler Hotel is a little like stepping into the closet of a stately, soft spoken, conservatively dressed grandmother and discovering a carefully hidden scrapbook that reveals a very different woman than you thought you knew. Decades old photos and yellowed newspaper clippings reveal the seemingly bland dowager to have once been the type of woman your mother warned you against. There had been a time when she wore six-inch stiletto heels adorned with rhinestones, too short a dress and revealed too much cleavage, exploding through the fabric of her blouse like twin volcanoes spewing lava. She was the woman who would seduce you, use you and get you to thank her even as she broke your heart.

The Statler lives on in Cleveland on Euclid Avenue just off Playhouse Square, and the renovated building houses beautifully appointed upscale apartments. Before the current incarnation, the Statler was an office building—sturdy, with suites to meet the needs of any business that chose to rent there, but nothing that would likely get the attention of a casual passerby. And before that, the Statler had been that aging dowager whose conservative appearance belied a youth of wild abandon and illegal activity.

CHAPTER 1
OMERTA AND BIG ANGIE

The Statler Hotel was young, vital and the destination of choice for men of power when a pair of touring cars pulled up in front of the hotel and eleven well-dressed men—their custom tailored suits concealing both their bulging muscles and their holstered handguns—stepped into the early morning air. It was December 5, 1928, and the time was 4:30 in the morning. Their presence would prove surprising, though it should not have been. The first time such men were known to have met at the hotel was when a young man named Angelo Lonardo was being honored as the newest member of what would become known as La Cosa Nostra—Our Thing.

In fact, so much happened in the Statler in its stately but audaciously wicked early years that it deserves a chapter of its own, a chapter that begins with a dagger, a gun and the oath of Omerta.

Angelo Lonardo had always known some of the dirty little secrets of the Statler Hotel, though he did not reveal them for the first time until he spoke of them before the U.S. Senate in 1988. By then he was seventy-seven years old. He was also a rarity—a former underboss of the Cleveland organized crime family who would eventually die in bed from natural causes at the age of ninety-five despite having become one of the FBI's most important informants. As he remembered the Statler, it's so important to start with his career as a bad guy:

June 11, 1930 photo of
Angelo Lonardo and
Judge James B. Ruhl.
*Courtesy Cleveland State
University Cleveland Press
Collection.*

*When I was "made"—or became a member of La Cosa Nostra—I went
through an initiation ceremony. I was invited into a room at the Statler
Hotel in Cleveland and asked if I knew what I was doing there. You
naturally say, "No." Present were John Scalish, the acting boss; Tony
Milano, the underboss; John DeMarco, a capo; and Frank Brancato. They
explained to me that I had been proposed to be made a member of La Cosa
Nostra and defined the rules and regulations of the organization. They told
me that you cannot fool around with narcotics; you cannot own a house
of prostitution or have prostitutes working for you; you cannot fool around
with a woman that's married to a member of La Cosa Nostra; and that
whatever illegal activity you engage in, you have to report to the boss and
receive permission to engage in that activity. After I was told the rules, I
was asked if I still wanted to join the organization. One can still leave at
that time, but the person usually accepts. In my case, I joined and became a
member of La Cosa Nostra.*

*Once you accept the rules of membership, they lift a cloth off a table;
underneath is a gun and a dagger. You are told that you now live and die
with the dagger and the gun. You die that way, and you live that way. You
are then given a card with a picture of a saint on it. The card is placed*

Everybody Loved the Statler

Angelo Lonardo. December 9, 1977. *Courtesy Cleveland State University Cleveland Press Collection.*

in the palms of your hands and lit. You shake the burning card back and forth until it is burned down to ashes. They then pinch your finger to draw blood, and then everyone gives you a kiss on the cheek and says, "You are now a member."

I later learned that to be proposed for membership in La Cosa Nostra you would have to have killed someone and stood up to the pressure of police scrutiny. Today, you don't have to kill to be a member but just prove yourself worthy by keeping your mouth shut, or by being a "stand up" guy. However, if you are called upon to kill someone, you have to be prepared to do it.

In my case, my father [Joseph Lonardo, former boss of the Cleveland family] *was murdered by Salvatore Todaro in 1927. In revenge, my cousin, Dominic Sospirato, and I killed Todaro. This is one of the reasons that I was proposed for membership in La Cosa Nostra.*

Lonardo never did say if there was a luncheon or other celebration of his new status, though the Statler food service was always considered excellent. Then, over the years, it was obvious that the mob enjoyed the hotel, such as would be seen as 1928 came to an end and the Statler unwittingly hosted the first national gathering of the leaders of organized crime.

11

CHAPTER 2

THE "GRAND COUNCIL OF THE MAFIA" — OR SOMETHING

It was 4:30 in the morning of December 5, 1928, when Patrolman Frank Osowski made what was to have been his last pass of the Statler Hotel before returning to the station. Had it been a few hours earlier, the two touring cars that unloaded eleven male passengers would have seemed like the vehicles groups of tourists routinely hired to transport them to and from area nightclubs and restaurants. Had it been a few hours later, when most of the guests had arisen from bed and enjoyed their breakfast, it might have seemed that a routine meeting was taking place. The problem was that downtown Cleveland had a rhythm to its year, and the men who entered the Statler under the watchful eyes of the uniformed officer did not fit.

The seven-hundred-room Statler, along with the Hollenden, Winton and Cleveland Hotels, was a primary upscale establishment for well-heeled tourists, business executives having meetings in the city and special events. There were elaborate wedding receptions, anniversary celebrations and other events that utilized ball rooms, party rooms, society orchestras and caterers who understood how to impress families for whom cost was never a concern. These were also events attended by society columnists and photographers who immortalized the attendees in the *Press*, the *News*, the *Leader* and the *Plain Dealer*. Black society—and Cleveland had wealth even among those who struggled against the city's racism—met at other locations where the events were covered by the *Call & Post*. But for everyone, the rhythm was the same.

Frank Milano. August 2, 1930.
*Courtesy Cleveland State University
Cleveland Press Collection.*

Weddings were events scheduled around college graduations, so June and December were both popular months. However, these were usually weekend events and certainly not something for which an all-male group would be arriving at 4:30 in the morning.

Conventions were common between September and June, but most people had no interest in business travel in December when Officer Osowski saw the touring cars. All he could tell for certain was that something was wrong, though he had no idea what.

Certainly the men who emerged from the two touring cars were appropriately dressed for the Statler. Their suits were expensive; their shirts appeared to be silk; their shoes were of high quality; and what jewelry they wore—watches, stickpins and cufflinks—all appeared to cost far more than the average working man could afford. Their luggage, too, was of the same quality as that carried by the other guests.

Well-dressed men emerging from a pair of touring cars in the hour before sunrise didn't fit any of the expected arrivals. It was December, but they weren't coming for a Christmas party. And the way they emerged from the cars—stepping out, pausing to look first to one side and then the

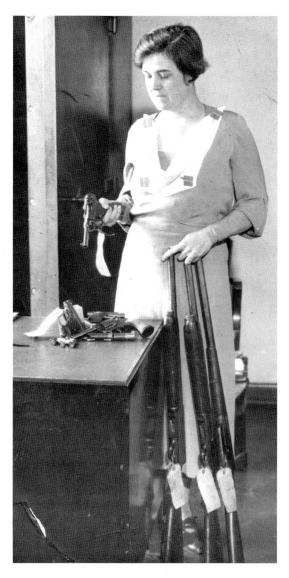

Marie Milano (Mrs. Frank). September 30, 1937. *Courtesy Cleveland State University Cleveland Press Collection.*

other, as though scouting the immediate area for potential danger—again was not typical.

The men undoubtedly noticed the uniformed police officer yet did not acknowledge his presence in any way, again a clue to something suspicious. The average person, honest or dishonest, coming into an unfamiliar area at an hour when the streets are mostly deserted, reacts to the presence of a uniform beat patrol officer. Some smile and visibly relax; some grow tense, looking about as though seeking an escape route; and some give a little wave, as though reassuring themselves that the officer's presence has nothing to do with them. Typically only professional criminals ignore a uniformed officer, knowing that at their level of dishonesty, the only people about whom they should be wary are detectives, distinctive in those days for their often rumpled business suits, trench coats and snap brim fedoras. Officer Osowski might as well have been invisible because of the way the arriving hotel guests ignored him.

A uniform patrol officer might be the lowest-paid member of a department, but such a man, walking a beat night after night in the same

Anthony Milano at a Senate
hearing on organized crime
(Kefauver Committee). January
19, 1951. *Courtesy Cleveland State
University Cleveland Press Collection.*

relatively deserted area was the best protection a community could have. He
would grow bored with his walk, instantly noticing the slightest change, and
in Osowski's case, acting on it. "The men looked both ways and pulled their
hats down as they entered the hotel," Osowski later testified, a gesture of
men on the alert for danger while avoiding being recognized.

Patrolman Osowski entered the Statler, lingering in the lobby. Again he
was invisible, just another cop perhaps getting an extra buck or two for
providing security before daybreak. The men checked in, signed the register
and went to their rooms. Osowski went to the desk and copied their names
as well as the names of others that had arrived earlier in the evening. He
paid special attention to the guests in suites on the second to the sixth floors
since the eleven arrivals seemed to have clustered their rooms on those
floors and other guests, having arrived earlier, had names that indicated
similar ethnic origins.

There would be twenty-three men visiting the hotel, and another seven
scattered among other locations for reasons never quite determined. Their
names seemed to indicate a Sicilian origin but, among them, seven came
from Chicago, nine from Brooklyn and there were two men each from St.

Angelo Porello's funeral (son of Rosario Porello). January 19, 1933. *Courtesy Cleveland State University Cleveland Press Collection.*

Louis and New Jersey. In addition, there were men from Tampa, Florida; Buffalo, New York; and Gary, Indiana.

Osowski returned to the police station and gave his superior officer, Lieutenant Kurt Gloeckner, the names, hotel room numbers, arrival times and all other information he had been able to obtain. Then the lieutenant took a few plainclothes detectives and went to the Statler to confirm what the patrolman had discovered. It was 10:00 a.m.

Lieutenant Gloeckner talked with the manager. He talked with the people working the front desk and the bellmen helping guests to and from their rooms. Finally he decided that all of the men who were staying in the same cluster the patrolman had noticed should be removed from the hotel and taken to the police station for questioning.

The lieutenant was sensitive to the men and women who stayed at the Statler, individuals who were often prominent in their home communities and either doing business in Cleveland or enjoying a vacation with their families. Even those who did not grace the society or business pages in their

Angelo Porello's funeral. *Courtesy Cleveland State University Cleveland Press Collection.*

local newspapers had money to spend that benefited the local economy. Any hint of danger or scandal could damage everyone.

Working quickly and quietly and avoiding violence despite the fact that eighteen of the men were carrying handguns, a group of seventy-five uniformed officers arrived, positioning themselves so that the visitors could be taken in the back without other guests noticing. Several patrol wagons handled the transportation.

(The location of the mobsters at the time of their arrest remains unclear. The total—twenty-three—is consistent in the press coverage. However, some reliable reports put them all in one room, indicating a meeting about to start. In addition to the weapons being carried by those arrested, thirteen guns were found in the room where the men had gathered following breakfast. The only Clevelander among them who was carrying a weapon was Sam Tilocca.)

The official reason for transporting the men to the police station for booking was an essentially bogus charge of being "suspicious persons." So far as was known, the only crimes that had been committed in the previous twenty-four hours were those committed by the police who failed to obtain warrants prior to searching either the men or the hotel rooms in which they had been staying.

The booking process had been an informational one. It provided the police with fingerprints, addresses and photographs that were taken both of individuals and groups. To the surprise of the detectives, it also yielded one wanted bad guy—Giuseppi Palmero, who was being sought by the Italian authorities for investigation into eight murders. He would not be allowed to make bail. His recent past also added no additional information about the reason for the gathering.

Newspaper reporters quickly learned enough about the men who had come to Cleveland to know that they were connected with organized crime. Some of the names were familiar; others were not. However, in order to sell more papers, the men arrested at the Statler were identified as being the "Grand Council of the Mafia," a definition that could neither be challenged nor proven.

As the press tried to sell more papers, the national importance of the Statler gathering was increasingly emphasized, though without corroboration from anyone involved. Certainly the Mafia was organizing on a national scale, though most people did not understand the way organized crime was developing in the United States. There were the Italians, of course, but there were also Jews from Eastern Europe and Irish. Cleveland had both the Mayfield Road Gang (Italian) and the Jewish Combination (Jewish, Greek and Italian), along with various factions seeking to consolidate power in one form or another. Among the men most concerned with ending territorial battles that made crime less efficient and less profitable than it might otherwise be were close friends Lucky Luciano (Italian) and Meyer Lansky (Jewish). Their efforts led to effective expansion into what became legal gambling in Havana, Cuba, and Las Vegas, Nevada, as well as the eventual takeover of the Teamsters Union. (Irish until Bill Presser, known derisively as "the fat Jew," moved himself into power while backing Jimmy Hoffa for national leadership.)

The battle to control corn sugar was considered one of the more likely reasons for the Statler gathering. Corn sugar was a key ingredient in making "moonshine." It was also the source of both violence and great profit. More important, within the Cleveland world of organized crime, the corn sugar issue involved two sets of brothers who came to Cleveland from the small town of Licata, Sicily.

The brothers—the Porellos and the Lonardos—began their working lives with the job most young, healthy males in Licata endured without leaving the community—back-breaking, lung-destroying physical labor in the sulfur mines. The difference between the two sets of brothers, who had also been childhood friends, and the other youths of Licata was that the Porellos and Lonardos had no intention of enduring gradually deteriorating health, premature aging and death. Instead, starting with the three-hundred-pound "Big Joe" Lonardo—the entrepreneur within his family and the young man who was expected to be successful as an immigrant if success was to be had in Cleveland—the two sets of brothers slowly emigrated from Licata.

"Big Joe" arrived in Cleveland just after 1900 and became a businessman, handling any product he could buy and sell for a profit, and a community activist. Bigotry against all ethnic groups had been a part of the immigrant experience in Cleveland and other American cities. The immigrants often had limited language skills, could not read the local papers and yet had an intense drive for personal success to benefit their children who were able to assimilate fairly quickly. Men like Joe Lonardo understood the community and the feeling that the adults were aliens to the city's culture. They provided goods and services familiar to the immigrants, whether running a neighborhood bar, meat market, grocery store or bakery or publishing newspapers in the language of the old country. They also understood the culture of the old country where a distrust of authority—both political and religious—was ingrained from centuries of abuse by either the church or the state. Sicily was an area where a patron/client relationship had developed out of necessity, and when the people came to the United States, the belief prevailed that nothing had changed. The result was that each new wave of immigrant was unlikely to trust the police, allowing the corrupt among the earlier arrivals to take advantage of the fears of their newly immigrated countrymen.

"Big Joe" Lonardo thrived as his family and friends knew he would. He built a legitimate business in the nickel trade, a metal increasingly in demand for use in various commercial and scientific processes. It was chemically inert, had a high melting point and its uses—including for plating—were just beginning to be learned. How it functioned was of no interest to Lonardo. However, the business required his working with a number of small suppliers and markets, a business model that would hold him in good stead when Prohibition became the law and he moved into the higher profit areas of bootlegging. He had earlier brought his brother John to Cleveland and his brother Frank a short time later. They learned how to handle the suppliers

John Porello and Angelo Porello. July 28, 1930. *Courtesy Cleveland State University Cleveland Press Collection.*

and buyers for the nickel business, and Joe trusted them to handle a similar business model in the supply of the more profitable corn sugar, which is used in the manufacture of corn liquor.

There were ultimately believed to be hundreds of stills operating in the greater Cleveland area when the Lonardos began supplying them with corn sugar. The brothers priced their product competitively and delivered fairly, asking only loyalty in return. The bootleggers, whether large or small operators, understood that they were to work only with the Lonardos, making their payments on time and never selling excess corn sugar. Since there were neighborhoods where two or more stills were adjacent to one another on the same street, they were able to quickly identify any problems with what amounted to a rogue bootlegger.

Bootleggers who bought from the Lonardos soon realized that the rules Big Joe established were inviolable. The punishments were swift and certain.

Angelo "Chink" Bottaro stole a quantity of corn sugar, and when his corpse was found, there were several bullets in his head. Others thought they could relocate without paying past due bills. They would inevitably be located and then an anonymous telephone call would be made to the police alerting them to where the dead beat's body could be found.

The Lonardos did not like killing but murder proved to be an effective business tool. It was also increasingly the first choice as men decided they could take on the Lonardos and others without building an adequate organization to keep alive. The result was that in 1925, three years before the Statler gathering, Cleveland was ninth in the nation in the number of deaths by "unnatural causes." Five years after that national gathering, Cleveland was third in the nation in homicides.

The Lonardos recognized that they needed more individuals they could trust as part of their organization. This was when Joe Lonardo decided he would be safest with one of his childhood friends from Licata, a man who shared his past and his hunger for success and also understood the problems inherent in bootlegging. He chose Joe Porello who, along with his brothers, had followed their old friends to Cleveland.

The violence was either ignored by Lonardo's rivals or the risks of muscling into the same business were seen as worth taking. Whatever the case, as the violence increased, so did the rivals' activity, including from the once trusted friend from Licata, Joe Porello.

Joe Porello was an opportunist, not an entrepreneur. He was "muscle" who was trusted by Joe Lonardo to help him enforce the rules of the Lonardo sugar sales.

Porello may not have been a businessman but several of his brothers were. They studied the corn sugar operation as it functioned in Cleveland, saving their money until they could begin a corn sugar business of their own. Then Joe Porello and his brothers began a rival operation in the Woodland area where they were able to quietly take control of some of the stills.

Then Joe Porello and his brothers went into business against the Lonardos. It was two years before the Statler meeting.

The Lonardos and the Porellos began a business war meant to give each side a chance to win through the consolidation of interests. The small suppliers understood that they would have to have a business relationship with only one of the two groups of brothers. If they handled themselves wrong, made the wrong alliance or acted other than in the interest of the brothers with whom they had been working in the past, there would be a bombing, a shooting and/or a beating.

The Lonardos were the more successful of the two groups of brothers because of Joe Lonardo's skills and the fact that he had been working in the business longer than any of his rivals. The Lonardos had reached a point where their business was generating $5,000 a week in profits, an amount that exceeded the gross profit of many legitimate corporations. Violence was limited, and it seemed to Joe that he could leave the business leadership to his brother John, a man who was completely honest though rather dumb, and travel home to Sicily for what would prove to be a six months' vacation.

John Lonardo never stole a dime from the business entrusted to him by his brother, Joe, but he could not keep the Porellos from taking more and more of the customers. By the time Joe returned from visiting his mother and cousins, the stolen business was so great that it had to be stopped. This should have met all-out war between the two groups, but Joe could not bring himself to start attacking the brothers he had known from the old country. Instead, Joe decided that the Lonardos and the Porellos would sit down and negotiate the return of the stolen business. What they had not counted on was the brief investigation into the murders of Yorkell and Brownstein, a pair of loser thugs whose lives and deaths never should have influenced the corn sugar wars.

CHAPTER 3

YORKELL & BROWNSTEIN? WEREN'T THEY ON STAGE LIKE ABBOTT & COSTELLO?

Ernest Yorkell and Jack Brownstein had names that sounded like a second-rate vaudeville comedy act, though Yorkell, a man who could look as though he was being violent when standing still, had spent part of his youth traveling with a circus side show. He wasn't billed as a thug when he and Brownstein came to Cleveland to take advantage of what they perceived to be a war over control of the city's bootlegging. Instead he would perform as "Young Hercules," taking advantage of his physical strength.

Brownstein was a man considered acceptable to bring home to meet your parents. He was allegedly a jewelry salesman from Philadelphia, and if anyone questioned why such a sophisticated dresser like Jack was would travel with a Neanderthal like Yorkell, the presumption was for protection from jewel thieves.

Yorkell and Brownstein were operating a scam in a city they did not understand. They had previously worked in Buffalo and Pittsburgh, with Cleveland the third city in which they decided to operate. They figured that since no one was likely to know for which local mob figure "muscle" might be employed, if they walked into a bootleg establishment and acted tough, they could get money and have the owner's rival blamed.

The extortion racket was a simple one. The two men would walk into a business, and then Brownstein would go to the owner and explain he had to pay up or die. Supposedly the threat had extra impact because the threat was made by Brownstein. The danger lurked in the hard-edged, looming Yorkell—or so everyone thought until the two came to Cleveland.

Oddly, it was the threat that caused the bootleggers to know the men were worth ignoring. No one made threats in the bootleg era. You came, took your money and left. If money wasn't provided, you might be bombed, you might be beaten or you might be tossed down the steps. Threats were for amateurs, and the two men from Philadelphia were certainly that.

The exact order of the extortion threats is uncertain, though it is known that James "Shimmy" Patton who ran the Harvard Club was targeted. Patton was so tough that when the famed Elliot Ness was Cleveland safety director, Patton held him and other lawmen at bay while making certain his guests, including kidnapper and murderer Alvin Karpis, slipped out the club's back door, taking the gambling equipment with them. The would-be extortionists were a joke to him.

Also not paying was Thomas J. McGinty, owner of Lake County's Mounds Club among other businesses. But the most ridiculous attempt at obtaining money came when the men entered Club Madrid and approached Phil Selznick about giving them four hundred dollars. He laughed in their faces, and it was then that the two would-be extortionists realized that not only were they failures, they had no money for food and shelter. Instead of demanding money, they asked if they could have a loan of ten dollars. Again they were refused.

On October 7, 1927, Yorkell and Brownstein initiated what presumably was their "Plan B" if the extortion racket failed them in Cleveland. Exactly what they had in mind is unknown. They had been chatting up a waitress and, perhaps making one last effort to impress someone—*anyone*—in Cleveland, they told her they were going out and would return with $5,000—or they would not return at all.

It is not known where the two extortionists went or who they threatened. What is known is that their corpses were found in a place called Amber Park. But it was not that they were dead that was so curious. The men had been tightly bound with clothesline before being shot several times. It was more than a murder, though. It appeared to the investigating officers and the coroner that the killer or killers had taken their time, shooting the men in the head and the body the way a teenager might take a .22 and plink at beer cans. The deaths seemed pleasure killings, as though someone had turned off the lights on a particularly obnoxious comedy team that had performed the same routine once too often.

The police did not care about the loss of the out-of-town extortionists, though they went through the motions of an investigation they knew from the start would go nowhere.

CHAPTER 4
A FUNNY THING HAPPENED ON THE WAY TO THE HOTEL

There was a certain etiquette to the killing of a rival. The murder should not be anticipated—the reason so many high-level mob hits occurred after the victim had been feted with good food, fine wine and the best cigars prior to two or more killers entering where the target had been eating, shooting him quickly so he would die almost unaware. The murder would also not take place in circumstances where men loyal to the target might defend their employer, shooting the killers and perhaps everyone else involved. Assassination was about eliminating a perceived obstacle. It was not meant to be combat.

The Lonardo brothers routinely traveled with trusted "hired companions," a term the newspapers often used for loyal bodyguards. At the time they were seeking to regain their lost business, there were two bodyguards who should have accompanied them. Unfortunately the men were considered suspects in the shooting of Yorkell and Brownstein. They would eventually be released without a trial, but they were temporarily being retained by the Cleveland Police. It was the ideal moment for the Porellos to agree to a sit-down in the card room in the back of a barbershop owned by the Porellos.

The negotiations to which the Lonardos agreed were traditional. Normally it would involve the men who had the dispute and their bodyguards. However, with the Lonardos' two most trusted men still in jail during the investigation into the Yorkell and Brownstein murders, and with the Porellos foregoing their own bodyguards, everything seemed as friendly as a mob business meeting could be.

John Porello and his mother at James Porello's funeral. July 31, 1930. *Courtesy Cleveland State University Cleveland Press Collection.*

The Porellos owned a barber shop that had a back room where men would gather around a table, playing cards, and talking. Sometimes the games were matters of friendship, though a "friendly wager" could lead to pots of hundreds of dollars or more for each hand. And at other times the backroom, the cards and the sitting together was a nonviolent way to remain calm and focused while seeking to settle a dispute, which was taking place when the Lonardos came by.

Joe and John Lonardo shared their concerns about what had happened during John's absence, telling the Porellos what they thought should be done to set matters right. The Porellos would hear none of it. They were not responsible for Lonardo losses.

On October 13, 1927, the Lonardos decided there would be no more talk. They had been wronged by their countrymen, brothers who were longtime friends. Had they known one another under different circumstances, they might have gone to war. But the Lonardos did not want violence; they wanted the customers they felt the Porellos had stolen from them, and they wanted them immediately.

The problem was that the Porellos had assimilated into the American mob culture more completely than the Lonardos. Angelo Porello was not going to have anyone dictate to him how to run his business. Instead, when the Lonardos went to the barbershop to see Angelo Porello, they found him standing alone in the backroom by the heavy wooden table on which the men usually played cards.

The Lonardos entered from the front of the shop, passing the chairs and going toward the inner doorway when Angelo suddenly dropped behind the wooden table. At the same moment, two gunmen working for the Porellos came up behind the Lonardo brothers and fired several rounds in each. Joe and John Lonardo were dead before they could react. There were no witnesses, and when it came to the Cleveland Police and organized crime battles, if there were no witnesses, there was no crime to fully investigate. The detectives looked at the scene, talked with Angelo, talked with the

Joe Porello's funeral. July 10, 1930. *Courtesy Cleveland State University Cleveland Press Collection.*

Lonardo family and decided that there was no link between the barbershop and the murder other than where the shooting took place.

Within weeks, Angelo Porello emerged from the carnage as the new king of the corn sugar suppliers. He also declared himself to be the new leader—capo—of the Cleveland mob. It was a job he expected to hold for life. He just did not anticipate how short that life would prove to be.

PARTY TIME AT THE STATLER

Angelo Porello basked in his new position, and a little more than a year after John and Joe Lonardo's deaths, he and his lieutenant, Sam Tilocco, invited mob figures from around the country to gather at the Statler Hotel. All arrangements had been made for them. Most would stay at the Statler, the site of the meeting. Others, apparently by their own choice, were scattered about the city. In the end, the interviews with the twenty-three from the Statler revealed to Detective Captain Emmett Potts the presumed whereabouts of the others, allowing him to arrest four of them. Three more men, their names unknown, had come to the city for the meeting but were registered at one of the city's most expensive hotels enough distance away from the Statler that they were able to flee the area before they could be identified or questioned.

Detective Captain Potts also took upon himself the task of acting as liaison between the department and the press that day. There were many questions about the validity of the arrests or the crimes that may have been committed. Potts admitted that it was illegal for any Ohio law enforcement officers to enter someone's residence without a warrant. The men were in hotel rooms and the fact that many were armed added to suspicions about them, but as the law had been interpreted at that time, a hotel room was classified as a residence for the person staying in it. What mattered was that the meeting was recorded and the men present were identified. Still the question remained—why were they there?

There have always been two "histories" of members of organized crime—the truth and what was believed to be true because the story made an important point. For example, in 1909, New York City police officer Joseph Petrosino was part of a criminal investigation involving the New York City Police, U.S. immigration officials and Italian immigration officials. They were working to understand the Sicilian Mafia and its involvement with New York's Black Hand.

Joe Porello's funeral. *Courtesy Cleveland State University Cleveland Press Collection.*

Petrosino gained permission to travel to Palermo to meet with the Sicilian police who agreed to open their files to him. They had full identities of the men who had come to America to commit crimes, hiding behind aliases and false backgrounds.

The Sicilian police educated Petrosino in their world of organized crime, and he helped them by coordinating the arrest in the United States of a man they were seeking. The fugitive from Italian justice was a member of the Camorra, a Naples-based secret society similar to the Mafia, but his lack of familiarity with the United States enabled the New York authorities to find him for their Italian counterparts.

The cooperation among the Americans and the Italians outraged the mob in both parts of the world. They decided to kill him when he went to Palermo in 1909.

The plot was simple. In March of 1909, with the officer in Palermo, an anonymous message was sent to him asking him to meet an informant under a statue in the Piazza Marina on March 12. He went to the statue

Ottavio Porello (black shirt and hat) on July 28, 1930, just two days after the shooting of his brother. *Courtesy Cleveland State University Cleveland Press Collection.*

where three armed men, allegedly connected with New York's Black Hand, murdered him and fled.

That was truth. However, the way the assassination was carried out was too simple for men trying to show reality; they did not show enough disdain for the man who tried to uncover their secrets and make arrests on two continents. Soon the Mafia myth was that Petrosino had been murdered on the boat that was taking him to Italy. According to the story—told as fact though known to be false—Petrosino was sitting on the toilet, his pants down, when the boat was coming to the dock. The killer entered and shot him where he sat, an ultimate insult. It was also a story frequently repeated among organized crime members and their sympathizers in New York.

There were other myths, of course. In Cleveland, one of these had to do with the corruption of the Cleveland Police detectives who regularly interacted with leaders of organized crime based on Mayfield Road. The story concerned two murders on July 5, 1930, and the victims were men connected with the Statler meeting fiasco.

The Porellos had made their power grab at a time when the most influential men in organized crime were looking to work more closely together. The killing of the Lonardos, the declaration that they were the new leaders and then the failure to provide a safe, quiet, private environment for the Statler meeting all led to men who might once have supported the Porellos to back off from such involvement. While before they had a thousand or more small-scale bootleggers providing them with income, they suddenly were losing political and business support.

Joe Porello was fairly certain where he could go to regain at least some of the prestige—not to mention the income—of the past. On July 5, 1930, he and Sam Tilocca arranged to go to the social club and saloon at 12601 Mayfield Road to meet with Frank Milano.

Cleveland had more than one "Little Italy" during this time—locations where men had settled after coming from one or another village. Where they settled was determined by their level of skill in the workplace. Some were physical laborers; some were doctors and lawyers; some owned successful businesses; and some sold whatever they could from horse carts.

Mayfield Road, now in the heart of University Circle's vast cultural and educational institutions, was the heart of the violent Mayfield Road Gang. Some of whose members would eventually help create the gambling mecca of Las Vegas, and others would be part of what became known as the Cleveland Syndicate. The act of coming to the Milano headquarters was as foolish as when the Lonardos went to the Porello barber shop.

Sam Tilocca and Joe Porello entered the social club where Milano, John Angersola, Alfred "Big Al" Plizzi and Charles Colletti were waiting. At 2:30 p.m., shots were heard and Joe Porello died on the floor with three bullets in his head. It was Tilocca who was the problem and whose death helped create the myth.

The execution of Tilocca was not as effective as that of Porello. Five bullets entered Tilocca's body, none killing him instantly. He fell and began crawling toward the door. Milano and the others watched, apparently enjoying what, to them, was a show. Closer and closer Tilocca pulled himself toward the sidewalk and the new car he had parked on the street. Finally he reached Mayfield Road, his body outside the social club, and there he died.

Fact was that the police arrived, and though the men known to be present were ignored, Frank Milano was investigated. The police expressed surprise that the tavern existed on Mayfield Road and even greater surprise that Frank had a home *next door*. The fact that both had existed for several years was not mentioned in the newspaper accounts.

Death of Ray and Rosario Porello. February 27, 1932. *Courtesy Cleveland State University Cleveland Press Collection.*

Everyone went through the motions of a real criminal investigation. Frank Milano's home was visited by the police, who dutifully noted a cache of automatic rifles and shotguns, ammunition, slot machines, cases of whiskey and beer and account books detailing expenses such as money paid to politicians, police and anyone else who might cause a problem.

As was typical in Cleveland in that period—men whose political achievements would result in their being honored by one association or another, voted into high office and often allowed to live and die with a carefully crafted, thoroughly bogus autobiography—Ray T. Miller made headlines by noting the findings in the Milano home. He was county prosecutor at the time with plans to eventually run for mayor, a position he would win because of his self-declared integrity. He also looked at the records, information that could send many of the city's most prominent men to jail, and announced that the records were "valuable." However—and there was always a "however" when it came to the tap dance of bribed officials trying to earn their regular payments from the mob, unspecified legal reasons made their return to Milano imperative—they could not be used in a criminal or civil case.

While the noninvestigation was unfolding, the Mayfield Road Gang finished what it had begun with the shooting of Joe Porello. James Porello wanted lamb chops for Sunday dinner, and as he stood in the butcher shop, his plans were radically altered by a shotgun blast through the window. He was buried three weeks after Joe's funeral.

Raymond and Rosario were murdered while playing blackjack with friends. They had tried to hide from their enemies by going on a Catholic retreat, a safe but boring escape that caused them to return to the streets. Finally, in September of 1932, the once powerful Angelo Porello was arrested and jailed for operating one small still.

So what was the myth? One story involved a murder inside the Venetian Restaurant on Mayfield Road. It was run by Frank Milano, and the Milano brothers were the notorious leaders of the Mayfield Road Gang. The mobster threatened the Milanos as he started into the restaurant, and one of the brothers pulled a gun and shot the man.

As the story was told, the mobster did not die instantly. Instead he dropped to the ground, bleeding and desperate. He pulled himself through the door

Funeral of Ray and Rosario Porello. *Courtesy Cleveland State University Cleveland Press Collection.*

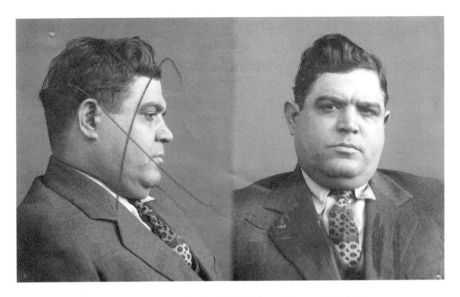

Sam Tolocca. July 6, 1930. *Courtesy Cleveland Public Library Photograph Collection.*

and back onto the sidewalk where he died in full view of numerous passersby, at least one of whom called the police.

The Milano brothers made no effort to remove the body or clean the blood. In their mind, the man had gotten what he deserved and there was nothing more to be done about it. Unfortunately the detectives did not see it that way.

According to the Milano myth, the handling of the murder was proof that the police were on the mob's payroll. The lead investigator raised hell with the Milanos for killing a man and letting him crawl out of the restaurant to die. "Next time keep the guy inside," one of the detectives was alleged to have said. "You kill him in your restaurant and no one cares. If he is in front, we have to investigate. We might even have to arrest someone."

The "proof" of the problem, again according to the myth, came when Frank Milano, one of the brothers present at the murder and the one suspected of pulling the trigger, had to flee the country to avoid prosecution. The year was 1935 and Frank moved to Mexico where he stayed for many years, though he eventually died of natural causes in Las Vegas. The part about Frank moving to Mexico was true because he would not be extradited to the United States yet he could quietly slip back and forth across the border to conduct business and see friends. However, he was never indicted for the murder. Frank had to flee Cleveland to avoid prosecution for income tax evasion. The myth was meant to once again degrade the image of law enforcement.

The story of the Statler meeting developed what appears to be its own myth. According to most sources, the December gathering was the first meeting of leaders of organized crime from throughout the United States. Certainly the men attending were either of great prominence or rising rapidly in the ranks of their cities' organized criminals. For example, Brooklyn, New York's Joe Profaci was present and arguably the most important visitor, ultimately founding what became known as the Colombo Mafia family. The Gambino family sent Vincent Mangano. Giuseppe "Hop Toad" Giunta and Pasqualino "Patsy" Lolardo came from Chicago. Lolardo was considered a man in the mob's equivalent of the diplomatic service, though how respected he really was can be debated. He was murdered a month after the Cleveland convention.

One other story about the meeting that never really happened was that it was supposed to be either the planning meeting or the first meeting (both stories are frequently told) of what became known as the Mafia National Ruling Commission. This had long been the shared dream of Charles "Lucky" Luciano (Italian) and Meyer Lansky (Jewish), close friends who felt it was time to stop the numerous murders and deadly power plays between and within the various Mafia families. They also wanted to apply modern business practices to crime. Joining them were Al Capone in Chicago, Frank Milano of Cleveland and Brooklyn's Joe Profaci.

The future that might have been explored during the Statler gathering became unimportant to men who were angry about being invited to Cleveland, then being arrested by the police. Such arrests showed poor planning on the part of Porello and hinted that he lacked the power to influence the police in his home town.

Joe Porello desperately tried to right the mistakes that had been made. He contacted family members and friends until he had enough money to cover the rather high bail of every mobster who had been arrested at the Statler. It was an approach that also prevented the police from learning more about their backgrounds than was already known. Only a few hours passed between the time the men were arrested and the time they had to be released, further proof of the power of the mob. The only man who was retained in Cleveland was Giuseppi Palmero from New Jersey, and before bail could be made for him, the police learned there was a warrant for his arrest for the murders in Italy. All others returned home. It was not the Statler's finest hour.

CHAPTER 5

AND ONE MORE STATLER STORY

The Statler was a hotel whose mission was to serve the public in the most professional manner possible. It was the place to take an honored guest even if that guest was being honored by being allowed to take an oath with a gun, a dagger and the swearing of Omerta. It was a place to hold a meeting even if those attending considered assassination to be one of those effective business tricks taught at Harvard University, if any of the professors thought of it before the mob. But there was also a presumption that, when it came to the Statler staff, every man and woman was above reproach. Even among those at the lowest end of the pay scale—the maids, the busboys and the like—no one would consider taking so much as a penny from a guest's room.

It was because of this attitude that to work for the Statler was to be working among the elite within the service industry, and that the new busboy was largely ignored. He was a wandering sort, or so it seemed; the year was 1937, and the Great Depression turned many young men into nomads seeking whatever better paying job might exist for them in the next town, the next city or the next state.

Bob Murray—as the new busboy identified himself when he was hired—was the type of familiar stranger restaurant and hotel employees encountered during the later years of the Great Depression. A guy like Murray, unattached, moving about the country in search of whatever opportunities might exist, routinely took jobs as busboy and dishwasher. The jobs didn't pay much, so men like Murray were always on the lookout for either a cheaper cost of living (his Cleveland hotel was $1.50 a week) or a higher-paying job. His time in Manhattan had not proven fruitful, though he did better in Washington, D.C., and Philadelphia. Sometimes he traveled by train and at other times by bus. He never said how he got to Cleveland, though he may have saved even more money by hitchhiking. He always knew, like other young men who traveled similarly, that a walk into the downtown area would lead to a restaurant or hotel job. Despite the Depression, such work was readily available.

Murray was different from the usual dishwasher/busboy who came to work in the Statler kitchen. Henrietta Koscianski, a nineteen-year-old Cleveland girl who had long worked as a pantry maid in the hotel, was the first to notice, in large part because she was the object of much of his attention. And it's not like Henrietta was without male attention wherever she went in the city. With her clean-scrubbed looks, her white starched blouse and a figure that even the most conservative clothing could not hide, men frequently wanted to spend time with her.

The new busboy also appreciated her figure, and she thought he was coming on to her when he said he was an artist and wanted to sketch her. He didn't try to take her anywhere; he just got his paper and pencil so she could pose while they took a break from work.

Henrietta and the other kitchen help quickly saw that Murray was not pretending. First there was the white soap carving he enjoyed while he sat in the kitchen during the restaurant's slow times. This was not unusual in itself; white soap carving having become a popular national hobby thanks to new forms of business marketing that had started approximately nine years earlier.

That year, 1924, had been the year that advertising innovators such as Henry Bern devised ways to help Proctor & Gamble develop approaches to not only selling more soap but P&G brands specifically.

First there was the creation of the National Soap Sculpture Competition in White Soap, which was an annual event attracting efforts by thousands of Americans. Bars of soap had long been used as multipurpose cleaning tools. The full bar would be used in the same manner bars of soap are used today. However, for cleaning furniture and other uses where the bar was not effective, a knife would be used to chip small pieces of soap to be mixed with water, and the soapy liquid could then be used for cleaning.

The problem faced by Henry Bern was that most people bought whatever soap they saw in the store. Some of it was good. Other types did a poor job of cleaning. Even when soap began to be offered in both granulated and flaked forms, washing was not simple and brand loyalty was almost nonexistent.

Robert Irwin (aka Robert Murray) after his arrest. *Courtesy Cleveland Public Library Photograph Collection.*

It was Bern who created such contemporary approaches as having a product present a popular radio show. In 1933, Procter & Gamble was trying to sell its Oxydol, a soap product, as the one consistently reliable soap product for washing clothes. This was when Bern agreed to have P&G underwrite a new type of entertainment—the original radio serial. On Monday, December 4, 1933, at 3 o'clock in the afternoon, the NBC Red Radio Network introduced *Oxydol's Own Ma Perkins*, the first of what would come to be known as soap operas and a show that remained on the air until 1960.

The new marketing efforts affected Cleveland as they did other cities throughout the United States. There were many neighborhoods in the city where you could walk the streets on summer afternoons when radios were turned up loud and the windows were open to take advantage of any breeze only to find that you never missed a minute of *Oxydol's Own Ma Perkins*—so popular was it. But it was the P&G soap-carving contests that created what was for a time the most popular hobby in America, or so Bern would have you believe as he both promoted and helped judge the entries.

Winners would win a number of different prizes, from cash to having their entry bronzed and placed in a special museum exhibit. And when he wasn't trying to sketch the buxom pantry maid, Bob Murray let it be known that he had won one of the contests. That was why he was practicing either on soap or on the ice he had to chop for the guests whenever he wasn't working or sketching.

Henrietta Koscianski was fascinated by her new co-worker, and she got a chance to study his face while sitting still as he sketched her. The night had been slow, and the lack of many customers that gave Murray a chance to sketch Koscianski also gave her a chance to slip upstairs in the hotel to find a friend who often kept magazines to read during breaks. That night, by chance, the co-worker had one of the popular true detective magazines.

Pre-World War II America was a time when most Americans lived in rural communities and in isolation from one another. Radio had only started to become a viable form of entertainment on a national basis in the late 1920s. Movies were popular, as were newsreels that enabled people living lives that would probably never allow for travel—whether to another state or another country—to visually experience other places and cultures. They also provided stories of villains traveling America, sometimes eluding local law enforcement and sometimes being caught, either surrendering peacefully or refusing to be taken alive.

Equally popular were special-interest magazines devoted to true-crime stories—*Headquarters Detective* and *Inside Detective* being among the more popular ones. The covers were fairly consistent with images—artist renderings for some and photos of posed models for others—depicting everything from a police officer making an arrest to female hostages, bound and gagged, while their kidnappers shot at law enforcement officers coming to the rescue.

Within the magazines were stories about one or another bad guy's crime spree and how a detective heroically tracked him down. There were stories of historical crimes, and most important, there were stories about criminals who had not yet been captured. These were men and sometimes women whose identities were known and whose photographs or artists' renderings were published along with details about the person's past, why he or she was wanted and where the person might be hiding. It was the equivalent of contemporary shows such as *America's Most Wanted* and the traditional, "low tech" posting of wanted posters in post offices throughout the country.

Henrietta Koslianski, Statler Hotel pantry girl. June 28, 1937. *Courtesy Cleveland State University Cleveland Press Collection.*

One of the other Statler employees had the latest edition of a true detective magazine that had the story of Robert Irwin, a fugitive since Easter Sunday listed as being sought by the New York City Police Department.

Henrietta read the brief story of Irwin with both horror and amusement. The horror was because of the depravity of his crimes; the amusement was because the picture resembled the Statler's new busboy.

The story in the detective magazine was of a triple murder that occurred in an apartment in the West 50s area known as Beekman Hill. The victims were twenty-year-old Veronica Gedeon; her mother, Mary; and a deaf boarder. The crime scene revealed that the mother, who had been slicing vegetables in preparation for an Easter Sunday meal, struggled before being killed. The boarder, a deaf man, had been left alone, sleeping soundly through both the older woman's fight for life and the death of Veronica, who arrived at the apartment at 3:00 a.m. The killer, who had once rented the room in which the current boarder was sleeping, took the additional life only because he was afraid the man might have heard or seen him prior to falling asleep.

There were numerous ironies to the murders that fascinated Henrietta the night she found the magazine. The first was the younger victim, photographer's model Veronica "Ronnie" Gedeon. (Robert Irwin never wanted his three victims dead. "I only wanted to kill Ethel," the married older sister he thought was still living in the apartment. "I loved her.")

The most frequently available jobs during the Depression came from posing for images looked down upon by respectable people. These included nudes and lingerie shots, whether for erotic enjoyment or to sell products. Ronnie Gedeon did it all, including having been "kidnapped," "killed" and otherwise exposed to various forms of mayhem when she posed for the same true detective magazines that eventually carried the story of her murder. It was work her mother apparently tolerated, perhaps encouraged for the extra income it brought the family, but her estranged father hated it. He told the police and the press that "She was wild!"—a product of a rotten American system in which "Children laugh at their parents." And he knew of what he was speaking. For a while, he was a suspect when a number of erotic magazines, though none containing his daughter's picture, were found in the back of his upholstery shop.

Veronica was also a lousy victim who had been fired a day or two before she was strangled because, according to the art editor, her facial expression looked wrong—for someone who was being strangled.

The killer, who later confessed to reporters for the *Chicago Herald & Examiner* who provided him with a defense attorney and newspaper space to tell his story, explained that he had gone to the Gedeon apartment to see Ethel Gedeon Kudnor, who he had loved from the time when he was a boarder. She had no such interest in him, which was the reason he was asked to leave the first time. The visit on Easter eve was to give him an opportunity to remove Ethel's head and turn it into a life mask. However, it was only after he had sketched Mary Gedeon that he learned Ethel did not live there. "The room turned blue with death," he told reporters and police. "I got her throat in my hands." The two fought, but Mary lacked the strength to effectively fight Irwin. He took her corpse into the bedroom, shoved it under the bed and then went into the kitchen to fix something to eat. Then he took a knife and a bar of white soap and did as Procter & Gamble so heavily advertised: he began carving a sculpture that he eventually left behind.

Veronica was drunk when she came home at 3:00 a.m. Sunday. She had no reason to think there was any danger, so she went to the bathroom, washed, creamed her face, curled her hair and rinsed out her stockings. She prepared for bed for an hour before Irwin confronted her.

Henrietta Koslianski, Statler Hotel pantry girl, on June 30, 1937 at the Newark airport where she is collecting her $1,000 reward for her part in the capture of Robert Irwin. *Courtesy Cleveland State University Cleveland Press Collection.*

A loyal Procter & Gamble customer, Irwin slipped the bar of soap he had been carving inside a cloth that he folded and held like a blackjack. Then he struck Veronica's head as hard as he could, the soap, weakened from his artistic endeavors, crumbling inside the cloth. He had hoped to kill her. Instead, she was just dazed, and he proceeded to strangle her.

It is uncertain just when the police decided that Robert Irwin was the likely suspect, though they quickly found the room he had rented the day before he killed the three victims. Once his name had been published in the New York papers, numerous people came forward who said they had known him.

The White House knew of Irwin because President Herbert Hoover had received a bust created by Irwin when he was a student of Lozado Taft, the noted Chicago sculptor. And while his sketches of women such as Henrietta were straight forward, other sketches he made seemed to show great anger toward women, including turning their heads into fanged snakes.

Irwin was also known in Los Angeles where he had worked for a while in a wax works, always trying to master all areas of art.

But it was in New York where Irwin's artistic endeavors took a perverted twist to which a number of psychiatrists alerted the police in those days before patient privacy laws. Irwin had been hospitalized more than once, most shockingly for trying to remove his genitals. The twenty-nine-year-old man had normal sexual desires, and he felt that their frequency and intensity, though no different than what was experienced by other men his age, limited his pursuing his true calling as an artist. Remove the genitals and he could focus full time on sculpture and drawing. He thought a surgeon would help him. Instead he spent time in both the psychiatric ward of New York's Bellevue Hospital as well as in the Rockland State Hospital for the Criminally Insane.

By the time Henrietta was reading about Irwin, he was being called the Mad Sculptor and Ethel Gedeon Kudnor was under constant police protection. The police thought Irwin was still in New York, perhaps hiding in one of the art museums. They also took the soap sculpture they had recovered and showed it to advertising executive Henry Bern, assuming he was the national expert. It was of no help, though knowing the identity of the probable killer meant his history as a champion soap carver (or whatever they called past winners) would reveal a little more of his past.

There was certainly no connection with Bob Murray, the reason the pantry maid decided to tease him.

The story was lurid, sexy (with the illustrations from Veronica's nude modeling work as well as the more discrete negligee images) and so far away that Henrietta was certain that it had no connection with Cleveland. The similarity between Robert Irwin and Bob Murray was obvious, but lots of people looked a little like one another, especially when compared with the less-than-perfect likeness of pulp magazine reproduction. That was why on Friday, two days after Murray had sketched her, Henrietta teased Murray by asking him if he had ever heard of Robert Irwin. As she suspected, he said he hadn't. Not many Clevelanders had followed the story if they didn't read the detective magazines.

It was not until midnight Friday that Henrietta Koscianski realized that Robert Irwin and Bob Murray were the same man. That was why he was always sketching; that was why he was always sculpting; and that was why he was so proficient with an ice pick, the tool he used to kill the boarder in the Gedeon apartment. She alerted the police, but by then he had fled. His locker was empty, and his hotel room had been abandoned. However, he realized he could not continue a life on the run, which is the reason he called the Chicago newspaper. He ironically chose the rival of the *Chicago Tribune*, the newspaper that had been the model for the Charlie MacArthur and Ben Hecht play *The Front Page*, which told about a murderer being hidden in the paper until the reporters get an exclusive story. The *Tribune* staff didn't believe Irwin was real, and so they lost the scoop.

Later, when Murray was positively identified as Irwin, and Irwin was behind bars, the Statler Hotel pantry maid told reporters she felt "like 5 cents" for not having said something sooner. She could not conceive of the fact that a murder in New York might have a connection with someone living, no matter how briefly, in Cleveland, and that both factors could somehow involve the beautiful, respected Statler Hotel. But for a hotel that was a favorite for meals and meetings with the mob, having a notorious employee should not have seemed that shocking a coincidence.

PART 2

AND IN
OTHER AREAS
OF THE CITY

CHAPTER 6

"MINOR" FELONIES AND OCCASIONAL MISDEMEANORS

The late Allen Friedman was an organizer for the Teamsters, brother-in-law of Bill Presser and uncle of Jackie Presser. The Pressers both led the union. Allen worked behind the scenes, carrying bribes to politicians, smashing heads during strikes when he stood on line as a "slugger" and committing arson when necessary.

Friedman was known for his aggression, his fearlessness and his behind-the-scenes efforts on behalf of both the Pressers and Jimmy Hoffa. But during many hours of interviews, the eccentric side was revealed. For example, he took this author to the Cleveland Fire Department at 1645 Superior, one of the newer buildings in the area. Later, when we were sitting in the living room of the apartment he shared with one of his daughters, he said, "That used to be a court annex." Friedman related. "When Jackie was on trial, all the evidence against him was in the annex in the judge's office. Bill and I didn't think Jackie was strong enough to handle jail time so Bill asked me to burn down the building to destroy the evidence. I had this big jar of a phosphorous compound some guy had given me, and I put some of that on the roof before starting the fire inside the building. The guy who got it for me said it was perfect for arson because it made a fire super hot when the phosphorous was hit by water. The firemen wet it down without knowing what was happening, and the steel girders just melted."

"Did you use it much?" I asked.

Bill Presser. *Courtesy Cleveland State University Cleveland Press Collection.*

"I had it for years. Every time I had to burn someplace, I'd take a spoonful of the stuff and toss it in the toilet. I knew it was good when it started to sizzle and steam, and that's when I'd flush it down the drain."

"I'm surprised it didn't eat holes in your pipes," I said, and that's when Allen froze, staring as if into the past. Then he turned his head toward his daughter's bedroom, called her name, and said, "Remember the pipe in the recreation room that kept leaking every time we flushed the toilet upstairs? I think I just figured out why."

Allen and friends both from the mob and the Teamsters were sitting around a table at the Winking Lizard in Bainbridge, not far from Cleveland. Allen had suffered a heart attack and remained a chain smoker. The other men had one or another condition that led them all to be discussing their mortality. They were talking about where they wanted to be buried, and Allen was adamant that it should be someplace far away from where anyone who knew him would look, and he didn't want the grave easily identified. It seems that the final insult he, the Pressers and other Teamster leaders would use on a longtime enemy was to go to the grave, unzip his pants and pee on the headstone. The conversation was triggered by such an action taken by one of their friends, Harold Friedman (no relation to Allen) of the Baker's Union.

The late Reuben Sturman was arguably the nation's leading distributor of hard-core pornography. Working originally from Cleveland, he became the richest and largest producer and distributor of pornography in the world.

While a longer story about him will be told later in the book, there is one vignette that belongs here.

It seems that in the early 1960s, a producer of child pornography brought his wares to Sturman's home in Shaker Heights, the wealthy Cleveland suburb. He wanted Sturman to handle the marketing of the material.

Sturman might be distributing films dealing with bestiality, female domination, oral sex and other acts—both kinky and obscene according to the laws of the day—but he would never allow children to be misused. Outraged, he whispered a request in the right ears, and the man who brought the child pornography was severely beaten, though far enough away from Sturman's business and residence so as not to seem connected.

Still reeling from what he had seen, Sturman asked others in the business if there really was a market for pictures of prepubescent boys and girls having sexual encounters. They made very clear that there was. That was a line Sturman would not cross, though he could not resist the thought that a variation might further line his pockets without making him feel like a moral degenerate.

Reuben Sturman entering federal court on July 20, 1978. *Courtesy Cleveland State University Cleveland Press Collection.*

Reuben Sturman. February 1980. *Courtesy Cleveland State University Cleveland Press Collection.*

According to sources active at the time, Sturman arranged for a trusted photographer to hire male and female models probably over the age of eighteen, the legal age to consent to such sex work. These were youths whose bodies were developing late enough that they had no pubic hair and the girls looked flat chested when photographed from the front. The models, all of whom seemed to just have entered their teens and thus were still years away from being legal, were then photographed in sexually explicit poses. The customers were convinced Sturman's distribution outlets had added kiddy porn. Law enforcement officers checking on the material quickly found that the models were consenting adults under the law.

And Sturman happily added to his wealth without troubling what he called his conscience.

The exact date is not known. The mob guys connected with the heist worked for Ray Ferritto out of Erie Pennsylvania. Ferritto, a gambler, murderer and burglar (along with having the occasional "straight" business investment) was temporarily in jail, and some of the men who worked for him decided to pull a heist in Cleveland. They apparently arrived with nothing in mind, driving to a truck stop where the drivers took relatively long breaks to eat, to rest and to catch up on paperwork. Sometimes the trucks were left with keys in them—sometimes not. And unless the load was clearly marked, no one passing by was certain what the trucker might be carrying.

Ferritto's intrepid entrepreneurs spotted a truck whose load, at least that portion they could see, consisted of large boxes marked "Pool T..." The second word, an employee of Ferritto later explained in an interview, could not be read other than the first letter.

One of the thieves realized what they had without having to risk being caught moving the boxes for a closer look. The truck was carrying pool tables, probably the good ones used in upscale bars, home recreation rooms and the like. They sold for about $4,000 and more, and so they could be sold "off the truck" for no less than $500 each and probably $1,000 apiece.

The thieves moved to the door, and one of their more skilled members got in the cab, started the engine and drove from the truck stop. Another man followed the trucker, and others stayed back long enough to be certain the rig's driver didn't show up in time to cause trouble. Then they all left, meeting again at an agreed-upon spot where they would unload the truck, load the pool tables into a rental and then take them to people they were certain would buy them.

The back was opened. Two of the men climbed inside and shifted the boxes for unloading. That was when the writing on the boxes became fully legible. That was also when the bad guys realized they needed more than initiative to make money illegally. They needed intelligence and planning. That was because the boxes hadn't been destined for a billiards parlor or similar location. Each box contained inexpensive, blow-up plastic pool toys.

The newsstand on East Ninth Street near the street known locally as Short Vincent was a bookie joint owned, at least in part, by Reuben Sturman. It held racks and racks of magazines of all types, and during the week, well-dressed men and women stopped by throughout the day to buy their favorites. This was the late 1950s and early 1960s when respectable men wore business suits and, usually, fedoras. Women wore hats, often with short veils, gloves, dresses that came below the knees and heels of appropriate height. Such proper dress was worn on weekends as well, so the elderly woman who entered the newsstand on a Saturday when I, too, was in the store was surprised by the hostility of the clerk.

My presence was a familiar one on weekends because I both knew the true source of revenue and the weekend etiquette for readers. I was learning to be a writer, and in addition to the handful of magazines I could afford to buy upon occasion, I tried to read as much as I could in the stores. On weekdays, my standing around and looking through the racks would have gotten a cold, "You gonna buy something, kid? This ain't no f...in' library." It would have been said even though I was careful to never damage the spine, dog-ear a page or otherwise make the magazine look less than pristine after I picked it up, read a few articles and/or short stories and returned it to the rack.

Reuben Sturman's distribution center at 207 East Sixty-fifth Street in Cleveland. May 6, 1969. *Courtesy Cleveland State University Cleveland Press Collection.*

Saturday was different. Saturday was when horse races were taking place throughout the United States; results were coming in on the store's race wire; and gamblers were calling in bets, bringing in bets and otherwise engaging in the transactions that assured a steady profit even when nothing was sold all week. Some kid wanting to just stand and read while the bookies worked with the real customers—hell, what was the harm? On Saturday, they didn't even glance to see that the magazines weren't damaged. On Saturday, it *was* a f...in' library.

So this dignified, well-dressed woman comes into the store, goes to the rack, picks up a magazine on up-scale suburban living, walks to the counter.

"Lady, what the hell do you want?" asked an angry clerk, a phone pressed against one ear as he made notes about either a bet or the incoming results of a race.

Taken aback, the woman stuttered and said, "The magazine. I want to pay for the magazine."

"For God's sake, lady, if that's all you want, take the magazine and get the hell out of here."

"But I haven't paid for it."

"Just get the hell out of here. What kind of a place do you think this is?"

CHAPTER 7
THE CLEVELAND JEWISH NAVY

Note: At least three cities, primarily Cleveland, Detroit, and Buffalo, lay claim to the Jewish Navy or "Little Jewish Navy," as it is sometimes called. All three may be correct to some degree, because all three cities had Jewish mobsters bringing high-quality Canadian liquor across Lake Erie and into the United States. However, of the three cities, Cleveland seemed to have the most valid claim, the most liquor smuggled and some of the most interesting characters of the Cleveland mob, especially the enormously powerful Moe Dalitz, who needs a chapter by himself. As to the "Big Jewish Navy," that term has been used in reference to operations in Detroit, Cleveland and, most frequently, parts of Florida.

Law enforcement officers called the makeshift, Jewish-mobster-owned flotilla of speedboats and yachts, a decommissioned submarine chaser and seemingly anything else that could be propelled across Lake Erie as the "Jewish Navy."

If it existed today, it would probably be part of a low-budget, politically incorrect comedy in which each boat has ten old Orthodox Jewish men (as a minion for prayer); each man would be dressed in a black hat, prayer shawl and black coat; and have a beard windblown from standing on the deck. Each also would have a shotgun in one hand and a prayer book in the other, ever vigilant for enemies as they sailed their vessels between Ontario, Canada, and lakefront cities such as Cleveland.

Six days they would sail, bringing the finest Canadian and European booze to the masses. On the seventh, they rest, perhaps contemplating side

Ben Nadel. *Courtesy Cleveland State University Cleveland Press Collection.*

businesses such as T-shirts on which there are sayings such as: "What would Moses Drink?" or "The Lord is my bootlegger. I shall never run dry" or "The Promised Land Casino. Be a part of the Miracle!"

That is the image the name Jewish Navy seems to conjure today: one that is humorous, outrageous and ultimately wrong. The reality was an ingenious smuggling operation for those customers seeking the same high-quality whiskey, gin and other beverages they enjoyed before Prohibition. And the front man for the Jewish Navy was a "schlub" of a "loser" named Ben Nadel.

Ben Nadel was a man of limited intellect, the type of small-minded thug of whom it might be said that the mold was broken before he was made. The fact that he was a dropout—hanging out on his home turf of the relatively upscale East 105th Street neighborhood where his family had moved from the Woodland area where he was born—meant little. He had been a poor student in the classroom, and he never tried to master the lessons of the streets. He was a no-achieving loner at a time when the cops and the criminals maintained a symbiotic relationship normally beneficial for everyone except their mutual victims.

The beat cops were underpaid; many worked two jobs. If they could afford a house, they often rented one or more rooms to make extra money for their families. Some accepted the low pay and extra efforts as the price they paid for pursuing a career they felt too honorable to ever besmirch by illegal actions. Others felt that the badge was the ticket to a better life. They ate their meals in restaurants that did not charge them. They grabbed snacks from fruit carts whose vendors deliberately looked the other way. And illegal businesses such as gambling joints magically became invisible so long as the beat cop could walk inside, receive an envelope of cash and walk on to the next business whose owner was paying what amounted to protection money.

The street kids were a part of this little-discussed economy of law enforcement. They were mostly learning the business of crime through actions such as breaking into freight cars on railroad sidings and merchandise-laden trucks parked for the night in warehouse lots. Youth just learning to steal on a level one step up from shoplifting grabbed what they could from wherever they could break in. However, they quickly learned to work with the police. Street cops and senior officers who knew about specific shipments of merchandise would alert the gangs to what was coming in, where it would be parked and what they wanted from it.

For example, in 1922, Cleveland radio station WHK (AM 1420) was one of the first in the country to be licensed. Other stations followed, along with the demand for the new, often expensive radios that defined a change in family entertainment. They were also easily fenced through pawnbrokers as well as businesses where the owners preferred to increase profits by buying some of his merchandise "off the truck" rather than from legitimate distributors. More important, a radio or two provided to key Cleveland Police officers serving the neighborhoods where the break-ins were planned assured the gangs would be invisible to law enforcement—except Ben Nadel.

Nadel resented the idea that a cop or anyone else could demand what amounted to a bribe from him when he was the one who spotted the trucks and freight cars; he was the one who broke inside; and he was the one who carted off the merchandise. The other kids in the neighborhood told him that he was being foolish, but he saw that they were not arrested and he assumed he would be immune as well. That was why he was surprised when he was arrested and convicted of "boxcar plundering," a minor charge that nonetheless carried—what could have been avoided—jail time.

Nadel had one revelation while doing time. He realized he needed a different business. Recreational drug use was becoming popular, and all the street kids knew the smaller-scale wholesale dealers whose drugs could then be sold at a profit on the streets. The problem, Ben quickly discovered, was that the dealers didn't trust him because of his poor relationship with the police, and the users didn't trust him for the same reason. Everyone who might do business with Nadel was concerned that they could get caught up in Ben's arrest should such an event occur again. The users would end up going "cold turkey" in jail and have to endure the shakes, the sweats and the cramps of withdrawal. The dealers would likely do hard time because of the quantity of drugs in their possession. He wasn't worth the risk.

Lloyd Mellett, the brother of murdered Canton editor, and Lloyd's son. *Courtesy Cleveland State University Cleveland Press Collection.*

Ben seemed to disappear from the streets of Cleveland for a while, at least so far as stories in the newspapers were concerned. He was undoubtedly still in the neighborhood as he grew into full adulthood, but he wasn't getting in obvious trouble. Then, unexpectedly, Ben reappeared. He was dressed like a respectable businessman with good clothes and more money in his pocket than ever before. He still came across as a thug, but there was no question that he had found a lucrative racket. Although Ben liked to give the impression he was in charge of the business, the Cleveland Syndicate had hired him for the Jewish Navy's Ontario-to-Cleveland activities.

Not that Ben understood he was a low-level "flunky" being given the look of somebody important so that, if the enterprise failed, he would be the one going to jail. It was the four leaders of the Cleveland Syndicate—Morris "Moe" Dalitz, Morris Kleinman, Louis Rothkopf and Sam Tucker—who really ran the Jewish Navy. They acquired the boats; they maintained the contacts in the United States and Canada; they planned the times when the shipments would be moved across Lake Erie and how the pickups would be handled; and they created an environment of little more than high pay and false flattery that kept Ben thinking he was not expendable.

The Jewish Navy was the supply line for the finest liquor available prior to Prohibition as well as the quality booze being distilled in countries such as Canada where Prohibition meant something quite different from the U.S. laws. Cleveland, like other cities, had pharmacies stocked with alcoholic beverages for sale. The American law allowed anyone to buy and drink liquor provided it was for medicinal purposes. The doctor was the person allowed to decide if a shot of whiskey would cure whatever ailed his patients, and most of the time it would. The trouble was that not every doctor would write a prescription and not every person who wanted legal liquor could afford the office visit.

Canada took a pragmatic view of Prohibition. The idea was to stop people from drinking to excess. Illness, absenteeism, family problems and other social issues were among the reasons Prohibition laws had been passed. But no one ever was hurt by owning an unopened bottle of booze; there was

Mellett murder scene with Pat McDermott present. *Courtesy Cleveland Public Library Photograph Collection.*

nothing wrong with alcohol if sober people made the beverages to assure the right quality for the marketplace; there was nothing wrong with alcohol if sober people filled the bottles and packaged them for shipping to other parts of the world; and there was nothing wrong with alcohol if sober people took it to the docks, loaded it on American boats, and received payment for their efforts. The pragmatic Canadian government assured that drinking would not be tolerated but the liquor industry would continue to enjoy the profits from the sale of its products.

The Cleveland mobsters who were the real brains and money behind the transportation of alcohol across Lake Erie had an unusual business. Their customers, often large-scale regional distributors supplying several nightclubs, speakeasies, gambling joints and similar businesses, wanted to be certain they would have a steady flow of booze. People planned their evenings' entertainment on visiting businesses where they could drink whatever they enjoyed in an atmosphere that combined fine food, quality entertainment and perhaps recreation in the form of "professional" women and casino-style gambling. They worried when the feds announced the arrest of any large-scale bootleg operation because it might mean an interruption in their business and the possibility of a rival stealing some of their customers.

The Jewish Navy provided two services, one tangible and the other psychological. First, it was the most reliable form of transport and distribution into the United States. And second, the syndicate learned to work with the media, creating "spin" that made even problems seem positive. Was one of their vessels intercepted by the feds, hundreds of cases of the highest-quality liquor taken from the vessel? It didn't matter, according to carefully spread rumors and misinformation. The feds missed dozens of other shipments that successfully crossed the water. The small loss would never hinder the Jewish Navy's ability to keep customers supplied, a reason for those businesses to not seek alternative means of smuggling liquor.

The feds played into the image of the Jewish Navy's dominance. They wanted their successes to seem much greater than they sometimes were. By not challenging the mob's implication about how much booze was successfully shipped, their intercepts seemed almost heroic in light of the formidable enemy they faced.

Ben Nadel may have been the front man for the Jewish Navy, but he was not one to travel with the ships. His primary activity was to have trucks and cars in locations along that portion of the Cleveland area coastline where a docking ship could be unloaded.

The best-known boat under Ben Nadel's "command" in 1925 was the *Ranger*, a sixty-five-foot cabin cruiser that could serve as a floating Great Lakes home for Ben and perhaps a dozen of his closest friends—if he had any. The *Ranger*, like the other vessels owned by the Jewish Navy, had been retrofitted to hold the largest possible volume of booze—680 cases in this instance—that would be taken to the drop-off point on the Huron River west of Cleveland.

Ben waited for the arrival of the *Ranger* with a truck and three cars, which would hold the ship's unloaded cargo of booze and have it driven to prearranged designations.

The problem was that the feds learned of the shipment and were waiting for the *Ranger* west of Cleveland at the mouth of the Huron River. It is not known what Ben may have thought first, when the boat was seized, and second, when he was not. Apparently no one saw him, revealing his relative unimportance once again.

The following year, the Jewish Navy's decommissioned submarine chaser was captured. The year of 1926 was also the time when the United States Department of Commerce released the information that the passageway used by the Jewish Navy was the source for two-thirds of all the quality liquor sent from Canada.

Ben Nadel fancied himself as someone important, as though he was in charge of everything instead of following orders. Worse, he thought he could be seen as an important player in the mob's activities, especially when it came to having some of their secrets revealed. It was an arrogance that would eventually cost him his life.

The downfall of Ben Nadel began in January 1925, with events that should have had nothing to do with him. The *Canton Daily News* was in a circulation war with the much larger *Canton Repository* when Don Mellett was hired to be business manager for the *Daily News*, a paper owned by former Ohio governor and one-time U.S. presidential candidate James M. Cox of Dayton, Ohio. Cox was aware of Mellett's previous work increasing business for the Scripps Howard *Akron Press*, and when he saw that Don was generating new interest in his Canton paper, Don was promoted to publisher. At the same time, Don's brother, Lloyd Mellett, became the Canton paper's crusading city editor, an approach to covering news new to the city.

Canton, Ohio, was one of those cities where everyone knew who was corrupt and what deals had been made to assure the corruption continued. It was a way of life that no one expected to change, and this reality was shared with the Mellett brothers soon after they were running the paper. The stories were horrifying.

Rear view of Donald Mellett's home with bullets in garage and kitchen. *Courtesy Cleveland Public Library Photograph Collection.*

For example, the man who was allegedly the most important of the Canton racketeers, a character named "Jumbo Crowley," had a close friend who was a surgeon with a long history of botching operations in Aultman Hospital. Instead of ending his privileges, the hospital board, pressured by Crowley, appointed the surgeon to chief of staff. He would have retained that respected, undeserved position had the Melletts not exposed what was taking place.

Another story the Melletts pursued had to do with mismanagement, corruption and abuse of prisoners by the police department. The evidence was so thorough that the mayor was forced to suspend the chief who was determined to get revenge.

Other critical areas of mismanaged public service were explored, including the board of education. Each article was carefully researched, hard hitting and accurate. Each one proved increasingly dangerous for Don Mellett, who was presumed to be in charge of his brother, the paper's city editor. That was why, though Louis Mellett was the man creating the headlines and determining the local coverage, Don would be marked for death.

And In Other Areas of the City

Threats began arriving regularly at the newspaper, but the general public was thrilled that someone was finally challenging the thoroughly corrupt status quo. The circulation of the *Canton Daily News* increased by several thousand readers, bringing it close to that of the rival *Canton Repository*, the pro-Republican Party newspaper and previously the paper with a far larger readership. But the *Repository* had no history of standing up to corruption, and the public loved the change. Not only were average citizens coming forward with ever more stories, but soon a man named Paul Kitzig contacted Lloyd Mellett to arrange a date to tell him about his personal knowledge of local corruption.

Kitzig's desire to talk was a major breakthrough. He was a known gangster himself, and the idea of him speaking frightened both the mob and the area's politicians enough that they arranged for a contract murder. The man chosen to kill Kitzig was Ben Rudner, a major bootlegger from nearby Massillon, Ohio, who hid his primary source of income within an auto accessory store he ran as a legitimate front.

Home of murdered editor Donald Mellett. *Courtesy Cleveland Public Library Photograph Collection.*

The Melletts investigated the Kitzig murder, determining that Rudner was the killer but also recognizing there would not be enough evidence to bring him to justice. They decided to print his name in the paper regardless of the circumstances, a clear message to the mob that the brothers knew far too much about Canton crime and politics.

It was Don Mellett who began to receive death threats and who found it necessary to hire guards. The mob did not understand the difference in the jobs the two brothers held. They did not realize that the city editor was the real power in this case, the man who coordinated the work of the reporters and chose how far to go with the various stories. Lloyd would live; Don had to die.

The angry Rudner contacted Steve Kascholk and Patrick Eugene McDermott, a pair of freelance mobsters who kept their consciences clean by never using them. They would do anything for a price, or so it was assumed. As it turned out, Kascholk actually had standards no one expected, fleeing from both Rudner and the city of Canton when what was supposed to be a beating turned into a request for murder.

Canton Police detective Floyd Streitenberger said he wanted Don Mellett beaten severely enough that he would drop the pursuit of the city's extensive corruption. He did not talk with Rudner directly but rather with another bootlegger named Louis Mazer, who also handled the negotiations with Kascholk and McDermott.

Apparently all the men were assuming that Don Mellett was to be beaten up until sometime not long before the publisher was confronted the night of July 16, 1926. Almost up until that moment, Rudner had been brooding over the indignities he felt he had suffered when the paper exposed him as a murderer. He ordered Kascholk and McDermott to kill the publisher, which was the reason Kascholk fled. McDermott, by contrast, seemed to feel that there was no reason he shouldn't get the money that would have been divided between them.

Detective Streitenberger also had none of Kascholk's such moral scruples. He joined McDermott in shooting Don when the publisher drove into his garage. One bullet entered his head above his left ear, killing him. A second bullet literally parted his wife's hair, though it went a fraction of an inch too high to enter her skull. It was never determined if they were trying to kill the couple or if one of the bullets meant for Mellett went astray.

It is uncertain whether officers with the Canton Police Department knew that one of their own murdered Mellett. Presumably they did not care. The homicide was not going to be investigated because the killer was seen as a hero to those who felt the city should operate as it had prior to the Mellett brothers' arrival.

What no one considered was that killing a reporter was different from killing a bootlegger or even a police officer. Other journalists became involved in the case and an independent investigator, Detective Ora Slater, was brought in to investigate. His work not only revealed the names of the killers, it also revealed that the Canton chief of police had been involved in both the planning and the aftermath of the murder, crimes that would result in his being sentenced to life in prison.

Detective Slater found evidence against Rudner, Streitenberger and McDermott but could not determine with certainty who had fired the fatal shot. He assumed it was McDermott, but before the man could be arrested, he managed to flee the area—and this was when Ben Nadel made his fatal mistake.

Nadel, always trying to ingratiate himself with bad guys throughout the Cleveland area, was approached by McDermott who was seeking to hide from the Slater investigation. Either Nadel was not bright enough to realize that this was one of the largest and most intense manhunts in the region, or he thought that he was especially heroic for helping a fugitive from justice. Certainly he ignored the fact that thousands of dollars in reward money was being offered for McDermott's capture and the act of hiding the man was a criminal offense more serious than any of his prior activities.

It was inevitable that McDermott would be arrested, and when he was, Ben Nadel faced criminal charges for harboring a fugitive.

McDermott was finally arrested, and when he was, Ben Nadel was charged with harboring a fugitive. He was convicted, released while he appealed, was convicted again, appealed again, and finally, on March 20, 1928, was told he would have to turn himself in to the sheriff to start serving his sentence. He had a short time to get his affairs in order, and he used that first day to make the rounds of the bars and gambling joints along Mayfield Road, the home territory of the notorious Mayfield Road Gang headed by Moe Dalitz, his former employer with the Jewish Navy. No longer caring to win anyone's favor, he complained bitterly about his life and the treatment he had received despite all his loyalty. The only person who cared about him was longtime friend and roommate Morris Goldman, though Goldman had not been connected with Nadel's helping McDermott.

The Cleveland Syndicate was alerted to the fact that Nadel was depressed, angry and bitter about returning to jail for a lengthy sentence. It was decided that Ben might be weak or stupid enough to tell the sheriff everything he knew about the Jewish Navy once he turned himself in. The members of the Cleveland Syndicate had kept themselves out of the media and had no intention of letting Nadel endanger their futures. Nadel had to die before he could talk.

The same March night that Nadel had been talking too much on Mayfield Road, he and Goldman left their rented room in which, in addition to their clothes, they had a small quantity of opium, a container of nitroglycerine and some dynamite percussion caps. The opium was presumably for personal enjoyment. The explosive was never explained.

What happened that evening is unknown. Their car was found parked on Lost Nation Road at 1:30 a.m., and the bodies of the two friends were found inside. Nadel had fourteen bullets in his body; Goldman had twelve.

Prohibition, itself, had just five more years of life. And the Jewish Navy became an almost forgotten story in the history of the Cleveland mob.

CHAPTER 8
SURE, THEY WERE DEADLY, BUT SOME HAD "SILLY-ASS" NAMES

Cleveland mobsters with names their mothers probably never gave them—in no particular order:

"High Pockets" Farinaci
Louis "Babe" Triscaro
Runt, the Jew Boy
One-Armed Gelfin
Morris "Mushy" Wexler
Alex "Alky" Miller
Dave "Honeyboy" Miller
Samuel "Gameboy" Miller
Alfred "Big Al" Polizzi
Charles "Cadillac Charley" Cavallaro
Dustin "Ducky" Corn (not a Clevelander but involved with the Cleveland Syndicate)
Pasquale "Butchie" Cisternino
Leo "The Lips" Moceri
Al "The Owl" Polizzi (also known as "Big Al")
Milton "Maishe" Rockman
Louis "Uncle Louie" Rothkopf
John "Peanuts" Tronolone
"Muscles Tony" Civetta

CHAPTER 9

CLEVELAND FOOTBALL'S DIRTY LITTLE SECRET

The problem with nostalgia and the Cleveland mob is that the elderly men and women looking back to a simpler time in their lives were never really involved with the bad guys, a major reason they have achieved old age. Mention Mickey McBride, for example, and—except for the longtime football buffs—many will speak lovingly of the comic strip *Toonerville Trolley* and the character Mickey "Himself" McGuire. Others remember yet another "Mickey," the five-year-old actor Mickey Rooney who appeared as the bully McGuire in more than fifty-five short features before aging out of the role. Always the image is of the tough-yet-endearing street kid struggling to succeed, and when it is mentioned that McBride, unlike Rooney and McGuire, was in the newspaper circulation business, the thought is of a Norman Rockwell cover for the *Saturday Evening Post*.

Mickey McBride was never part of a Kodak moment or a world where little boys stood on street corners hawking newspapers to passersby, sometimes working before and after school, sometimes spending the day shouting "Extra! Extra! Read all about it!" and then calling out that edition's new headline. The newsboys who worked for him rarely rose before sun-up in Cleveland's harsh winters, dressed in layers of raggedy-but-clean clothing lovingly mended by mothers who were both worried and proud or thought their future would be more Horatio Alger than Damon Runyan.

Sometimes this mythos would include a loyal dog trudging along beside the youth. Sometimes it might include a girl who admired the work ethic and determination she sensed would turn the industrious paperboy into an ideal husband and father. Instead, McBride and others in the circulation businesses were essentially gang leaders, not humanitarians. They sought the toughest street fighters they could find, boys willing to smash heads if necessary to gain the choicest corners for selling whatever newspaper circulation manager gave them.

Newspaper circulation determined many factors, from advertising revenue to community influence. A newspaper was often owned by someone trying to promote one political party or another, one candidate or another, one social cause or another. The greater the circulation, the greater the influence the owner could exert in the community.

Mickey McBride (left) with Paul Brown on December 27, 1948, after the Cleveland Browns had won three consecutive championships. *Courtesy Cleveland State University Cleveland Press Collection.*

Likewise, the more competing papers were unable to be distributed, the less their influence.

There were four primary English language newspapers in 1913 Cleveland when Arthur B. McBride arrived in the city. The morning *Leader* went head-to-head against the *Plain Dealer*, while the afternoon *News* fought for supremacy against the *Press*. Each was a champion for one or another political and social ideal, but no matter which members of the political or business community supported one or another paper, the fight for circulation dominance could be brutal. McBride, whose age at the time was probably twenty-seven but was often given as being as young as twenty-three, was a veteran of the Chicago newspaper circulation wars, working for William Randolph Hearst's *Chicago Evening American*.

Hearst had his employees combine a number of aggressive methods for making his newspapers succeed. The editorial content was weighted toward the sensational, the sexual and the violent. The ideal stories might involve the elite men in business and government cheating on their wives with women who were society leaders, the wives cheating on their husbands with men who were immigrant laborers and everyone carrying a weapon in order to kill/castrate/torture or otherwise engage in violence that could be followed by a lengthy, gossip-filled criminal trial. There were also the "yellow pages," a gimmick best known with the Hearst newspaper in San Francisco. Every Sunday there would be a "family education" feature in a section that was literally printed on yellow newsprint. For example, there might be an article on the women of Bora Bora carefully illustrated by a staff artist. Neither the writer nor the illustrator had ever traveled to Bora Bora, nor had they seen pictures or otherwise been acquainted with the place. However, the writer would create a compelling sociological study that might include the fact that the women engage in their various chores topless. There supposedly is nothing sexual about the information. It is presented as fact and illustrated

Mickey McBride. February 21, 1946. *Courtesy Cleveland State University Cleveland Press Collection.*

by drawings of women who look as though they could be contemporary pole dancers, at least from the waist up. Men delighted in their "education" from the Sunday paper, and teenage males were helped into puberty—all in the guise of Hearst educating the public.

In addition to the types of stories Hearst ran, men like McBride went out each day to knock on doors and try to get the public to buy it. The successful ones not only gained extensive new subscribers, they also battered the youths working for rival newspapers.

McBride would later tell the U.S. Senate's Kefauver Committee, which was investigating organized crime in Cleveland and other cities, that the job of circulation manager was simple. The paper had newsboys on various street corners throughout the circulation area. "They were chasing our boys off the corners," McBride said, making reference to the carriers working for the paper that lured him from Chicago, the *Cleveland News*.

It is difficult to understand what newspaper sales meant at the turn of the century, though it helps to see how much the job could pay. McBride, the circulation manager for the *News*, was treated with both the respect and the pay scale of a top general. He started in his job being paid $10,000 a year to organize the newsboys working for the *News*. This meant choosing strong young men comfortable fighting with fists, clubs, knives, chains and, when they could get them, handguns. They were the business equivalent of the street gang, and McBride's salary depended upon how well he organized his newsboys to avoid losing their corners to one or more violent rivals. Those who worked alone were usually boxers. For example, one teenager was a British immigrant—whose father was a heavy-drinking, probably alcoholic, stonecutter—sold the *Plain Dealer* from in front of the Southwest Grocery, not too many blocks from his uncle's plumbing shop where the family stayed when they first arrived in the United States.

The British kid started hawking papers wherever he could before he was old enough to enter school. As he grew older and tougher, training to become a professional boxer, he moved to corners where success meant he had to meet every physical challenge.

Leslie Townes Hope expected to win the Ohio State Boxing Amateurs Association title when he was sixteen—not that he was skilled enough to be cocky. All the boys with serious plans of a boxing career had the same self-assurance; it was the only way they could put in the long hours of school, training and fighting when necessary on the street.

There was one other problem for Hope, though. "Leslie" was a manly name in his native Eltham, England, but one that brought him ridicule in the

United States where it was mostly used when naming females. He changed his name to "Packy East," a name he considered right for a boxer. The first name was taken from the much admired fighter of the day, a man known as Packy West. The last name was taken to honor his high school—Cleveland's East High.

Packy East moved among school, fight training at Charly Marotta's boxing club on East 79th Street, and the East 105th Street corner in front of Southwest Grocery where he sold newspapers.

Perhaps it was the street fighting that made Packy East feel that his boxing career was certain. His first two fights were easily won, a fact that gave him confidence when he stepped into the ring with another teen named Happy Walsh. The man who came to be known as Bob Hope, a vaudevillian, actor, singer and, most famously, a comedian, told a *Plain Dealer* reporter years after he was an internationally known entertainer: "Never forgot my last fight…a guy by the name of Happy Walsh. They called him Happy because every time you hit him he smiled. We fought at Moose Hall. I gave him my Sunday punch. He smiled. Then everything turned black."

McBride, unlike teens such as Bob Hope, had reached what others might have considered the pinnacle of success when he was orchestrating a portion of the newspaper circulation wars on behalf of the *Cleveland News*. His $10,000 pay had the buying power of around $200,000 back then. And when McBride had built circulation from door to door canvassing, street-corner selling and forcing store owners to always carry the *News*, not the *Press*, he was given a raise to $15,000—well over a quarter-million dollars a year in today's purchasing power.

McBride's sales force consisted of tough guys, some trained boxers like the young Hope and others best described as dull-witted thugs. Ninth and Woodland, for example, was the corner for McBride-hire Alfred "Big Al" Polizzi, a Sicilian immigrant, the son of a blacksmith and eventually a major drug trafficker working with organized crime financial genius Meyer Lansky. Later Polizzi and his family moved to what might be called the new Little Italy, an area around Mayfield Road that ran from East 119 to East 125. It was there that Polizzi came to be known as the head of the organization called the Mayfield Road Mob, a group of men who would be instrumental in expanding gambling into Florida, Cuba and, most importantly, Nevada. He also went into separate business with his early mentor, McBride, with the two men developing much of the city of Coral Gables, Florida.

Morris Wexler was another young man who went to work for McBride during the newspaper wars. Wexler, known by everyone as "Mushy," brought Cleveland the famed Theatrical Grill on Vincent Street, the stretch between Sixth and Ninth Streets—actually a single, short block— known locally as Short Vincent. The Theatrical was a mob hangout as well as the place to come for entertainers such as Frank Sinatra when they either performed in Cleveland or were passing through the city. Across the street was a barber shop where the men who cut hair were elderly and obviously not making much money. The shoeshine "boy," on the other hand, was a punk from Little Italy whose custom-tailored suit and alligator shoes easily set him back a thousand dollars in the early 1960s when he was taking bets. An Italian restaurant in the same stretch had low-priced pasta dishes on the first floor and "professional" women working from the second floor. East Sixth formed the top of a "T" running from Euclid to Superior with a traditional magazine stand midway through the top. Milt Reitman had a camera store that drew an upscale clientele from area law firms, advertising agencies, corporate headquarters and the like. And Ninth Street, just off Vincent, had the Roxy, the last burlesque house in the downtown area.

But Mushy Wexler's success as a mob-connected restaurateur came after World War II as did his involvement in the development of Las Vegas. He first learned the realities of business, including the violent ways of competition, while selling newspapers and driving a newspaper delivery wagon for Mickey McBride.

The newspaper boys did not realize that they were being studied for the future by men such as McBride. All were tough guys, even Bob Hope, whose boxing record was less than stellar. The future comedian had worked out regularly to earn the right to be a prizefighter, and he had the courage to get into the ring against any opponent for whom a match had been arranged. He just wasn't very good at boxing at that level and found that a career in a different entertainment field was much more sensible.

Other men, like Wexler and Polizzi, were tough and comfortable with taking whatever physical risks were needed to succeed. Some went into the management side of illegal night spots and liquor joints during Prohibition. Others became enforcers, providing the muscle to keep illegitimate businesses from getting out of hand from unruly patrons or too aggressive cops. And still others acted as bodyguards for mob figures, bootleggers and large shipments of illegal alcohol.

Eventually there was a myth that future mob members, whether from among Cleveland's Jews, Irish or Italians, had gotten their start working in speak-easies. The truth was that under the direction of men such as Mickey

Mickey McBride
on the witness
stand during the
Kefauver hearings.
January 17, 1951.
*Courtesy Cleveland State
University Cleveland
Press Collection.*

McBride, they started as paper boys, albeit ones that Norman Rockwell would never have painted.

McBride was a man determined to increase his wealth even though his pay for his handling of the *News*'s circulation department was as much or more as that of many corporate executives. He loved the potential of the media and became interested in what was then known as a wire service. He invested in the Cleveland-based *Continental Press* and *Empire News*, which were being run by "Mushy" Wexler and his equally colorfully named brother-in-law Sam "Gameboy" Miller. Miller preferred breaking heads to touting races, left his share of the race wire to his brother-in-law and moved on to being a gambling casino troubleshooter for the Cleveland Syndicate.

It was summer 1962, and I was a smartass high school junior with a camera and a curiosity about Short Vincent. I left my parents' house with some excuse or another that sounded plausible, and because this was still the day of wired, dial-up telephones, there was no way to check where I might have gone.

Strangers were not unusual on Short Vincent back then, including nosy teenagers, because the Hollenden Hotel was only a few hundred feet away. The Hollenden was both upscale and had somewhat lower-priced rooms for business travelers and families on vacation. The restaurant was reasonably priced, with quality food enjoyed as much by locals who stopped for lunch or dinner as for the guests. In addition, the second floor was known to have what amounted to an after-hours joint, a place where all manner of illicit pastimes could be enjoyed when other businesses were closed.

I stood in the open doorway of a building that ran from Euclid to Vincent, taking pictures like a tourist though making certain I caught the shoeshine "boy" coming to work and the beautiful young women who entered the business that was family oriented in front and a place for a sexual experience on the second floor. I must have looked innocent enough to be of only limited concern yet suspicious enough to be confronted by three men I had never seen before. One, quite possibly the manager of the Theatrical at that time, informed me that he was the "mayor" of Short Vincent. Slightly behind and to one side of him was a second man whose suit coat bulged in a way that implied both regular trips to the gym and a shoulder holster that would have carried a revolver, a more trusted weapon than a contemporary automatic pistol at that time.

The third man reminded me of Chloe, the huge, powerful and seemingly retarded man-child who confronts Daffy Duck in some of the Warner Brothers cartoons of the 1940s and 1950s. Chloe was a lunkhead, a character both brutal and as out of control as a small child having a temper tantrum.

The mayor and the muscle stayed back. "Chloe" came directly to me and took my arm. "Let me break his arm," he said to the "mayor." "Let me break his arm."

"What are you doing here?" the "mayor" asked.

I don't remember what I said. I know I remained calm, curious and seemingly naïve. I also don't know if the "mayor" recognized I was avoiding the question or just was too stupid to know I had gone down the wrong street at the wrong time. I do remember that he suggested I go back to the hotel, presuming that I was a guest in the Hollenden.

For another moment a very disappointed Chloe looked from the "mayor" to me and back again. "Come on," he said. "Just let me break his arm." But by then the other two men had turned back to the entrance of the Theatrical, and Chloe knew he was supposed to follow and not take any further initiative when it came to my body and pain.

Mickey McBride during the Kefauver hearings. January 24, 1951. *Courtesy Cleveland State University Cleveland Press Collection.*

I had no idea how stupid I had been until I was reading the next day's newspaper. There had been a murder some time before the *Plain Dealer*'s first edition, a few hours after I had returned home. One of the thugs who worked for the club owners had been found dead, dumped head first into a trash can. I never did learn the victim's name, but the picture made clear who had died. It was Chloe.

SO, WHAT IS A RACE WIRE?

It was a Cincinnati Western Union Telegraph Company operator named John Payne who invented the race wire. For years the telegraph had been used to alert subscribers to the results of horse races throughout the country. Within a few minutes of a race, if the customer was near the telegrapher receiving the results, he would know if he had won or lost. This arrangement meant that gambling could be done based on races throughout the United States, not just in the city where the gambler was living. It also meant that

Western Union seemed to encourage behavior that some stockholders found improper and perhaps immoral. They demanded that Western Union stop involving itself in the racing industry.

Payne not only restored the use of the telegraph for the reporting of race results at the start of the twentieth century, but he also improved it to where it was impossible for a subscribing bookie to lose money on last minute bets.

The Payne Telegraph Service of Cincinnati began with two employees at each horse racetrack: one was the telegrapher who would send the results to all subscribers—handbook operators who were called "bookies"; the other employee was a spotter with a mirror.

The spotter would go to the race and position himself at the end of the track where he could learn instantly which horse had won. The telegrapher would be located within line of sight of the spotter's mirror. The moment the first horse raced across the finish line, the spotter would flash a signal to the telegrapher. It would tell him who had won and enable him to wire the results to the handbook operator subscribers.

Speed mattered. Other telegraph companies supplied horse race results but none were as fast as those using the Payne system. By getting the results to the subscribers first, even if only five minutes ahead of the others, the bookies could safely continue taking bets from their customers after the race was over. If a number of gamblers wanted to make last-minute bets on the horse that had already proven to be the winner, the bookies would know to refuse. By contrast, if the betting favorites were known to have lost, the bookies would take bets on those horses up to the moment when all the wire services reported the winner. In such an instance, every bet placed before the bookies had to admit the race had been won was clear profit.

How valuable was the Payne system? A man named Mont Tennes, infamous for his involvement in gambling, agreed in 1907 to pay for the exclusive use of the Payne system in Illinois. The rental, which sent the daily results to the train station in Forest Park where a special switchboard and lines coded to provide results to hundreds of handbooks and poolrooms, cost $300 a day. This was approximately $7,000 a day in contemporary value.

The mention of poolrooms has to be explained. Poolrooms and pool halls were not places men would visit in order to play the game of pool. They contained no tables and balls and no cue sticks or any of the other accessories of the game. Despite the misrepresentation of fact in a number of contemporary plays and movies, a poolroom was a place to gamble in those days. Pictures of pool halls that had been raided during the Depression showed signs with races and other events taking place around the country along with chalked results and tables where bets were taken. The game of pool was played in billiard halls. (The game was properly called billiards in those days.)

Gradually Tennes increased his income by gaining a monopoly on results—no one could receive horse race results by telephone or telegraph without paying Tennes 50 percent of his net receipts. This was still a highly profitable business for the independents, but it made Tennes extremely rich. There were violent attacks against him and his businesses, but others became interested in race wire operations. Some were investigators for the interstate commission. Most were rivals connected with various mob figures in Chicago, New York, Cleveland and elsewhere. The one of concern for this chapter was Mickey McBride.

The use of the racing wire jumpstarted a social phenomenon that followed World War I. Americans in large numbers became interested in gambling, especially placing bets on horses. The world of the casino was not yet an important part of the culture. Even early gambling meccas such as Miami, Florida, and Havana, Cuba, were focused largely on horse racing, and men who had been involved in the newspaper circulation wars began to develop products to serve them.

The wire service was for the bookies. In addition, men such as Chicago's Moe Annenberg learned circulation through creating their own gangs to dominate street corner sales and then became involved in publishing (e.g. in Annenberg's case, buying into the *Wisconsin News*). From there, it was a logical step to developing race wires—and from race wires to racing forms. These were essentially small, special-interest newspapers that grew increasingly complex with their financial success throughout the country. However, the racing forms always included where a race was taking place, the horses that were running and the horse's history with different track conditions. One person would place a bet based on the horse's name. Another person would check the track's condition, such as whether the horse would be running on mud, and then looked to see past success in such conditions.

A long-shot bet might be placed on a horse that had never won a race but was moving up in the field each time he ran. Or a long-shot bet might be for a horse that was always last, making the gambler think that the horse must be due for a break soon and the odds would make even a small bet pay a large profit.

There were racetrack touts who handicapped the horses and sold his knowledge and wisdom even though the gambler paying the tout probably knew as much about the particular race. And there were mob setups in which a certain horse would win and that fact was explained to key personnel.

(When FBI Director J. Edgar Hoover became a fan of horse racing, he was regularly photographed making two-dollar bets, the smallest amount possible at tracks throughout the country. Sometimes the horse won. Checking the bets made during a racing season would probably show Hoover broke even. What was not known was that a trusted FBI agent was quietly making bets of one hundred dollars or more in his own name for Hoover. Often the horses chosen were at the suggestion of mobster Frank Costello, who was an acquaintance of Hoover through mutual friend, columnist Walter Winchell. Those horses would always win.

Winning was seldom a matter of luck when bets were made for Hoover, of course. Sometimes the winning horses would be doped for speed. Sometimes the losing horses would be doped to reduce their speed. When veterinarians were able to test for dope, jockeys were bribed to hold their horses back just enough for the designated horse to win. That was a better arrangement because occasionally the doping would result in one of two circumstances that could potentially embarrass everyone. The horse might suddenly become confused and stop, though in at least one incident the horse dropped dead before finishing the race. Or the horse might start to run the wrong way, a not uncommon occurrence. Bribing jockeys was less risky.)

The gamblers seldom suspected a race was fixed, and even those who were suspicious tended to assume that it was their chosen horse that would win. They were hooked—the nation was hooked—and the men who had been part of the newspaper circulation wars began looking to create a national wire service that would include a publication like Annenberg's *Daily Race Form*.

McBride understood when he had a job too good to leave. He stayed with the *News* until 1930, employing a mixed bag of Jewish, Irish and Italian mobsters. Gameboy Miller and Mushy Wexler worked for him, of course, but so did "Big Al" Polizzi, Sammy Haas and Tommy McGinty. In addition, he helped with the business side of Frank and Tony Milano's Brotherhood Loan Company prior to Frank having to leave the city.

The Brotherhood Loan Company was the simplest type of profitable immigrant-assistance group. Most Cleveland immigrant groups had some sort of brotherhood or society limited to a particular neighborhood. These were often not unlike contemporary credit unions established to serve just the members of a church or specific denomination, employees of a hospital, law enforcement or any other designated group. Immigrants often held menial and seasonal jobs; they often did not speak enough English to understand financial matters; and they felt most comfortable talking with their fellow countrymen who lived in their neighborhood, spoke their language and understood their problems. Such organizations might offer traditional savings accounts, but the simplest and most profitable just loaned money.

The Brotherhood Loan Company provided a loan-only service, charging higher rates than what would have been paid if the people using the company had been comfortable going elsewhere. However, the Milanos knew that their countrymen did not feel comfortable in traditional financial institutions, and they knew that no matter how outrageous the terms for money loaned, there would be no complaints. If anything, the people would likely think they were getting a better deal.

The story of the wire service wars and the battle of the racing forms is one of Chicago, Miami and elsewhere and companies such as the Universal Publishing Company, the General News Bureau and the Nationwide News Service, among others. But it was not until the players bought out one another, went to jail for a related crime or were murdered that the story returned to a Cleveland focus and the creation of the Continental Press, established on July 25, 1942.

Prior to becoming a major investor in Continental Press, McBride had become known for utilizing his substantial wealth for a series of businesses. He had developed the motto "Nobody ever got rich on a salary," and in pursuit of that concept, he looked to investments that helped him prosper from public necessities such as housing and transportation. For example, when he resigned from the *News* in 1930 at the start of the Great Depression, he did so in part because he could rely on the income from apartment buildings he had previously purchased in the suburb of Lakewood. He also bought a construction company, and after leaving the newspaper, he began looking at the taxicab business.

Taxicabs were highly profitable for the owners. Personal car ownership had been too expensive for most people even before the stock market crash; taking streetcars to and from business appointments, using them to visit family and friends and for other purposes was not always practical. Cabs offered a comfortable, affordable way to get around the city on the rider's schedule. In addition, the cab business seemed in some ways to be similar to newspaper circulation.

There were several rival cab companies, with the two primary Cleveland ones being Zone Cab and Yellow Cab. Drivers split their fares with the owners, and while the owners paid for the equipment, the dispatching of the cars and other overhead, the companies usually made more money than the drivers.

The drivers and the owners looked upon the fight for fares in the same manner as newsboys once fought for the best street corner sites. It was all about being willing to smash heads, smash cars and intimidate potential passengers from hiring one's rival.

McBride made his first purchase by becoming majority owner of Zone Cab in 1931. A drivers' strike had been going on, and there was almost as much violence against the owners as against the rivals. McBride was comfortable with using strong-arm tactics more violent and sophisticated than anything the drivers had encountered. Not only did the strike end and the streets become quieter, McBride was praised for his business acumen. The newspapers wisely chose not to mention the fact that the mobsters who had been trained during the newspaper wars and honed their violence in speak-easies were available for whatever McBride needed.

Three years later, in 1934, McBride added Yellow Cab to the businesses he owned, combining it with Zone Cab in order to dominate the city's business. There were periodic battles with the Teamsters Union and with rival cab companies, but overall the business was stable and the profits made him even wealthier. However, his roots in newspapers and the race wires led him to take over the Continental Press Service in 1939.

There was no secret that the Continental Press Service was an integral part of frequently illegal gambling. In 1951, when the U.S. Senate Organized Crime Investigating Committee was looking into McBride's past involvement in such a crime as part of a nationwide effort to understand interstate activity, McBride said, "I never have been in a bookmaking joint in 25 years." Then he admitted that a race wire provided results such that "the news eventually went to the bookies," but the bookies got the news from local news services who were his clients. "I have nothing to do with selling to any bookmakers," claimed McBride.

According to McBride's Kefauver Committee 1951 testimony, he started a new business, the Continental Press, "on a modest bankroll of $20,000 purely out of sentiment and goodwill to provide a job for my brother-in-law, [Tom] Kelly."

From the Third Interim Report of the Special Committee to Investigate Organized Crime in Interstate Commerce, known as the Kefauver Committee, May 1, 1951:

Mickey McBride and the Majorettes. *Courtesy Cleveland State University Cleveland Press Collection.*

Arthur B. McBride, whose son is the nominal owner of Continental Press, described in some detail at the Cleveland hearing his key position in the distribution of gambling information to bookmakers for over a score of years through the wire service. His testimony will be considered in the section of this report dealing with the wire service. It should be noted here, however, that one of McBride's "tough boys" upon whom he depended during the days when he was involved in newspaper circulation and taxicab wars, was Morris "Mushy" Wexler. Mushy, like so many of McBride's former musclemen, now holds a key position in the distribution of wire service for Continental Press in the Ohio area through his ownership of the Empire News Service. Wexler could not be questioned as he evaded the service of a subpena, but in Ohio as elsewhere; although there is an attempted facade of respectability, the Empire News Service is primarily engaged in the distribution of gambling information to bookmakers...

McBride testified that the only reason he went into the business was to help his brother-in-law, [Thomas] *Kelly, and another old friend,*

[James] *Ragen. It was suggested by counsel for the committee that he could have loaned Kelly $20,000 and allowed Kelly to become the owner of the business but McBride said that he did not feel Kelly was sufficiently seasoned in business to be trusted with a loan of that size - this despite the fact that McBride had loaned similar amounts to known gangsters on at least two occasions and also despite the fact that when he did take the business over he had to trust Kelly to run it.*

McBride stayed in Continental until 1941. Then he sold out to Ragen.

The story continues with Ragen and Kelly operating Continental until 1943 when McBride says Ragen came to him and said that he simply had to have McBride or a member of McBride's family in the organization. Nobody has given a clear reason for this because McBride, in his testimony before the committee, said that he had not learned anything further about the business up to that time and he had neither the energy nor available time to give to it. McBride had a son, Edward, who at that time was overseas with the Armed Forces. Obviously Edward could not give any attention to the business. But for him McBride purchased a one-third interest for $50,000 which was paid out of McBride's share of the profits. Why McBride had to be brought into a business which was operating successfully and did not need capital is obscure unless it was to make McBride's powerful connections with John Angersola (King) and other important leaders of the underworld in Cleveland.

Continental Press Service continued to operate without serious trouble until about 1946. During this period Ragen and McBride operated it as partners and there is no indication on the record that during this period it was dominated by any out-and-out gangster element although, beyond any doubt, Continental Press enjoyed amicable relations with the gangsters who were building up large-scale bookmaking operations in the bigger cities of the country.

The most interesting example of the relationships among the gamblers, law enforcement and McBride's operation was John Fleming, a captain with the Cleveland Police Department who became a partner in McBride real estate deals. He was also on the Yellow Cab payroll until 1941.

McBride made certain that he used Captain Fleming in ways that would prevent investigations into wrongdoing. The captain's investment shares gave him $30,000 in Coral Gables real estate in a venture that included not only McBride but also Big Al Polizzi, who was well-known by law enforcement for his drug involvement. McBride also had Captain Fleming negotiate real estate deals with various mobsters.

Ultimately, it did not matter what crimes McBride committed. It did not matter what sources he used for his initial investment capital or whether his businesses were legal. Mickey McBride was the man behind what was once the most successful football team in sports—not just in Cleveland but the nation. Mickey McBride created the Cleveland Browns.

There will always be questions about McBride's decision to obtain a football franchise for Cleveland. Was this another opportunity to increase gambling earnings? Did he unreasonably think he might be able to influence the outcome of games in the manner that horse races could be manipulated? Or was McBride seriously interested in the future of the sport?

Ultimately, no one seemed to care as the full story unfolded.

Professional football was a haphazard affair in Cleveland during the 1920s and 1930s, the early years of the sport. The first team established to play under what was then the American Professional Football Association (the name later changed to the National Professional Football League), was the Cleveland Indians (not to be confused with the baseball team of the same name created in the same era and continuing to this day). Later Cleveland football teams would include the Bulldogs, the Panthers and the Rams, which won the NFL championship in 1924.

It was the Rams that became the first professional team to have loyal, consistent fans, albeit too few in number for any investor to take seriously. Clevelanders preferred the college game of amateur football even though only Western Reserve University (now Case-Western Reserve) had a somewhat skilled local college team. (Baldwin Wallace had the Yellow Jackets; John Carroll had the Blue Streaks; and Case Tech had the Rough Riders.)

The end of World War II saw the new Cleveland Rams, established in 1937, win nine of the ten games they played that year, clinching the NFL Western Division Title. Then, that December, 32,178 fans packed the old Cleveland Stadium (since replaced by the Cleveland Browns Stadium) to watch Cleveland beat the Washington Redskins 15–14.

The excitement of the championship game was enhanced by the celebrity status of quarterback Bob Waterfield, the husband of actress Jane Russell, who was as famous for her 38-D breasts (natural, not surgically enhanced) as she was for her acting skills. She had moved to Cleveland to be with her football-playing husband when she wasn't working on a movie. She also had the dubious honor of being introduced by Cleveland native Bob Hope, a man unable to ignore the actress's chest, as "The two and only Miss Russell."

And In Other Areas of the City

In an ironic sports move, the success of the Cleveland Rams led principal owner Daniel F. Reeves to reevaluate his team and the city in which they played. He felt that the harsh weather and the position of the stadium on the lakefront might limit the number of fans who showed up when the team had to play in inclement weather. He felt that a city with loyal fans but nice weather would enhance his ability to make money. He obtained permission from the NFL to take the name and the players to Los Angeles.

The move of the Cleveland Rams to California not only frustrated Clevelanders, it also upset McBride, who planned to buy the team if they stayed in Cleveland. Once he lost that opportunity, McBride wanted to create his own team and then go head-to-head against the Rams to prove he had Cleveland's best team.

Arthur McBride had become rich through his businesses and investments when the Rams moved west. In addition to his other property, McBride owned most of the parcels of retail and residential buildings along the north side of Lorain from West 117th to West 130th Streets. He also had land in other parts of Cleveland, Lakewood and Florida, savoring visiting his real estate the way some men enjoyed looking at paintings or rare postage stamps in order to relax.

McBride had always been aware of football gambling, but he supposedly became interested in the game itself when, in 1940, his son became a student at Notre Dame University, where football was part of the Holy Trinity of Father, Son and Quarterback, and God only rooted for the school's team. McBride also noted the tremendous gambling interest when he observed the reaction to the first College All-Star Game held in Chicago in 1934 in which the previous year's best college seniors played against the champions of the National Football League. The money gambled easily rivaled what was used when betting on horse racing.

McBride had little idea about various college coaches and their strengths and weaknesses. He just assumed that Notre Dame was at the top, along with their coach, Frank Leahy. It was probably more because of his awareness of Notre Dame than because he knew the best coaches. Whatever the case, McBride wanted Notre Dame's coach Frank Leahy to handle the team that would come to be known as the Browns. However, when that proved impossible, McBride went to John Dietrich, the longtime, highly respected sports columnist for the Cleveland *Plain Dealer*. Dietrich was a diehard Ohioan, and that meant that when he thought of football, he thought of Ohio State University in Columbus. The team was not the best in the country and neither was the coach, Paul Brown, but on any given day it would have been impossible to find anyone better. More important, Brown knew how to choose great players and how to organize a team to maximize player skills.

World War II was not yet over and the thirty-six-year-old Brown was on military leave from Ohio State, working as a coach for the team being fielded at the Great Lakes Naval Training Station. However, before called to the military, Brown had coached Ohio State to the 1942 national championship. He also was driven in his determination to have the best team he could assemble, only-half jokingly telling McBride "We will build a winner if it takes every cent you've got."

The money was more meaningful for Paul Brown than Clevelanders knew at the time. Coaching the Ohio State football team was arguably the most glamorous job in sports. Whoever held the job was the most popular faculty member on campus, extremely well paid and known throughout the country.

Brown had long considered coaching Ohio State to be the high point of his career, a goal he had fought to attain, proving his ability at Massillon High School before joining OSU and taking them to a national championship in 1942. Entering the military only meant a hiatus in a career to which he planned to return, coaching for the rest of his life.

McBride had nothing to offer except cash. He had never been a part of the world of football. Some of the businesses he owned were involved with gamblers on college football. He had discovered the almost addictive excitement of college ball when his son went to Notre Dame. But he had never been a serious fan. He did not know which college teams were unusually good and which were only average. He had no idea how to spot a brilliant player on a weak team or a weak player on a strong team. He also had little sense of who could be the most effective coach for a professional team. Worse, there was no professional team. He had not been able to purchase the Cleveland Rams. All he had was the money to hire players and a coach, the money to carry the team both during the war years and when the country was again at peace.

McBride had bribed enough talented men over the years to know that Paul Brown, for all his dreams, had a price, and if Mickey could determine what it was, Brown was the man who might give Cleveland its first and most successful professional football team. Finally, an agreement was reached in which Paul Brown, while in the military for however many months or years that might mean, would receive $1,000 a month in salary. (Note: In 1940, the average American salary was approximately $1,725 per year.) Then, as soon as the war was over and the players hired for the new team, Coach Brown would be paid $25,000 a year.

It is not known if McBride had any thoughts of a name for the team, but the new coach was so respected that soon everyone called the players "the Browns." His skills were also obvious from the first game the new team played. It was an exhibition game against the Brooklyn Dodgers (football) in the Akron Rubber Bowl. The new Browns won 35–20, and then went on to win fifty-two games from 1946 through 1949 in regular season play (there were three ties and four losses). However, it was 1948 that brought the most excitement to Cleveland with the Browns winning all fourteen games that they played.

The Cleveland Browns became the most admired football team in the nation, and Coach Paul Brown showed that the faith Mickey McBride had in him was justified. However, as low a profile as McBride maintained, he realized that he could not continue with his latest venture as long as he might desire. Cleveland had become a major target for the Kefauver Committee on organized crime, and McBride was in the midst of an investigation about which one Senate investigator said, "Because of the enormous wealth that passes through the hands of the Ohio gambling syndicate…I have become more or less convinced that if Ohio is not the financial capital of gangsterdom [*sic*], it is surely one of the best sources of easy money."

Mickey McBride was never charged with a crime; he was never convicted of a crime. He ran his businesses so they would provide a steady source of income, keeping a low-enough profile so no one challenged his years of involvement with organized crime and gambling in conjunction with his ownership of a football team that was a favorite of odds makers and gamblers throughout the country.

McBride sold the Cleveland Browns in 1953, receiving approximately $600,000, one-fifth of the sale price that would be achieved in a few years. It was a large profit, but he probably would have continued to hold the team as he held the real estate had it not been for the Kefauver Committee. The man who consorted with some of the most powerful mob figures of the day, a man who had made millions of dollars in businesses that included covers for illegal activities and a man who had gained his early success through the judicious use of often extreme violence was one of those rare figures who died of natural causes.

CHAPTER 10
A GOSSIPY LITTLE CLEVELAND BROWNS STORY

Over the years there have been stories told about the players and their lifestyles, investors in the team, sportscasters, sports writers and others connected directly or on the periphery. Perhaps the most interesting story that some claim is apocryphal; and others—allegedly better in the know—swear is truth.

A well-known bachelor sportswriter was in Las Vegas with one of the investors in the Cleveland Browns. The investor was well acquainted with a woman who worked in what might be considered loss prevention in one of the casinos. All gambling casinos are planned so that, over time, every player will lose money. There was one casino that had a large sign on the gaming floor that read, "Highest pay-off on the strip—94% of the time." It was a sign that excited many gamblers who quickly lined up at the nearby slots and began inserting coins, pulling handles and inserting more coins. They knew that the sign was true, that the payoff was the best on the strip. What the players never thought about was the fact that a 94 percent payoff meant that for every dollar gambled, the player was guaranteed to lose six cents.

Despite the reality of Las Vegas, hope is ever present and, for some of the high rollers, it is fueled by the occasional big win.

The intelligent gambler will take the big win and leave. The recreational intelligent gambler will continue to play after the win, stopping only when continued gambling has led to breaking even—going home with the same amount of money with which he/she entered the casino. As for the average

Vegas high roller, the right seduction can keep him at the tables, the slots and the cards until he not only loses all his big winnings, but he also empties his wallet, maxes his credit card and otherwise gives the casino a far greater return than would otherwise have been possible.

Prostitution is illegal in Las Vegas, though it is legal in most of the state. This does not mean it is unavailable; it's often "disguised" as an escort service where the young woman might be willing to independently negotiate an arrangement beyond a "date." However, the story related to the two Cleveland men involved both directly and indirectly with the Browns concerns a woman who was part of a casino's effort to keep as much money as possible.

A woman who became prominent for her philanthropy and social success in Cleveland was working for one of the Las Vegas casinos in a critical, discrete, yet no-holds-barred job. When a high roller showed signs of continuing to win or quitting play without losing, the woman was one of the employees who would walk over to the man. She might watch him play whatever game he is enjoying; she might wager a small amount herself (house money, though the player does not know this), becoming increasingly excited as he wins "for her"; she might touch his arm in a brief, intimate gesture; and she might talk with him, telling him how impressed she is. She will never say she works for the casino. It is likely she will not say she lives in Las Vegas; though if she does, it will always be in that part of the city that is "normal"—away from the strip. In any case, her only interest is in being with the man who is doing so well.

If the man at least loses all that he has won, the woman may leave with some excuse to keep him from knowing she was with him just to keep him playing. If the man wins and then wants to stop, a casino employee will come over and tell him that a special room has been reserved for him on the house. This is often a penthouse or other large suite and it truly is reserved for high rollers. The big-money gamblers who travel the world will be booked automatically into such a suite when they make reservations. These are men and women who gamble for the excitement of the play, not caring about winning. They predictably lose large sums and expect to do so. But for the occasional high roller who simply got lucky for a few hours, the complementary suite is meant to keep him luxuriating in the sensuality and excitement of the casino.

The woman who is working with the lucky high roller will tell him how impressed she is by what is happening. He has already been given free drinks over a long-enough time that the gambler has no idea that the house wants to weaken his resistance to common sense without him knowing that the casino staff wants him drunk. Now the woman might whisper that she has never heard of what is happening and has certainly never seen such a place, and she wonders if he would mind letting her come up to the suite with him so she can take a peak. Her job, if all goes well, is to spend whatever time it takes to keep him playing. If that means sleeping with him, she will do so. For the few hours necessary to preserve the casino's finances, he is the most important man in her life.

According to the story, one such woman was well-known by one of the eventual investors in the Cleveland Browns. How they met has never been mentioned; how they became friends is also not discussed. What is discussed is the fact that she was introduced to the successful sports media star from Cleveland and that the two apparently fell in love. She was single; he was single. She was ready to leave Las Vegas and the endless round of high rollers; he was ready for whatever fantasy he was certain she would fulfill (and may very well have).

The happy bridal couple settled in Cleveland, blending with society. He worked, and she stayed home or went with him to various events that were attended by the city's elite.

It was at one of these parties that an extremely wealthy businessman whose projects existed throughout the United States noticed the wife of the sports celebrity. He was married to a brilliant, capable businesswoman respected by all who knew her. However, it is presumed that she was less exciting than the Las Vegas transplant.

No one will say for certain what happened next. Was it a love affair? Was the woman a gold digger? Did the businessman prefer "boobs" to "brains?" Whatever the case, adultery was in the air, both the Las Vegas transplant and the businessman choosing to commit it with gusto.

The businessman's wife was humiliated; their children turned against him; and all he cared about was being able to live openly with his new love. That was when he offered the aging sports celebrity a chance to retire to Florida with $1 million (the figure most often cited). The sports personality had already lost his wife; agreeing to a divorce that would at least leave him wealthy and physically comfortable seemed the sensible next step.

Eventually everyone involved in the sordid affair either died or left Cleveland except the businessman and his wife. And in an effort (successful) to assure their acceptance among the city's elite, or at least those who consider one's wealth to be the key to social standing, portions of their money are routinely donated publicly to locations that will display their names, and privately to those who will keep him in politically connected deals.

Mickey McBride would have been proud.

MICKEY MCBRIDE'S
CLEVELAND BROWNS TAXI SQUAD

Football teams were allowed to have thirty-three men on their rosters. These were the best available, but good coaches like Paul Brown were able to spot young talent who could be nurtured into stardom with a year or two of seasoning. These were not men they could put on their rosters because they were not yet better than the regular players.

The problem for McBride and Brown was that if the up-and-coming players were not on the roster and thus the payroll, there might be another team, not as skilled as the Browns, willing to sacrifice winning by adding the rising talent. They would have them on their roster, and in a year or two the men would be the stars of the league. It was a potential problem that did not affect many players, but in an average year it was estimated that five such men would be desirable for Cleveland. The answer was the Taxi Squad.

The rules stated that a football player could only be paid by a team if he was on their roster. Thirty-three could be paid. The thirty-fourth could not. So what could be done?

Paul Brown identified the future stars for Mickey McBride. Then Mickey went to usually five men and asked them if they wanted to go to work for his taxicab company. The job was simple: They were on the cab company payroll; they would get to attend all the Cleveland Browns football games; and they would get to work out. What they would not have to do was get behind the wheel of a cab. Instead, they received a cab company salary on the cab company's payroll check while waiting in the wings for their chance on the football field. They were like the understudies of the Broadway stars, except that no one could ever show they caused a team's payroll to carry more than thirty-three young men for the playing field. The remaining five (on average) were the "taxi squad."

CHAPTER 11
MOE DALITZ: HE ALSO DIED OF NATURAL CAUSES

Moe Dalitz moved from Detroit to Cleveland in order to make money. He moved from Cleveland to Las Vegas to spend it. Along the way he bought and ran laundries, made killing for hire a profession with benefits, developed arguably the finest "rug joints" in the country, was among the brains behind and investors in the Jewish Navy and his organizational skills became the model on which Meyer Lansky based the running of New York rackets.

Quite probably, you have never heard of him.

Moe Dalitz was a man better known for his early years in Detroit and his later years in Las Vegas, Nevada, than his time in Cleveland, which were arguably the most violent, criminal and successful few years of his life. Detroit was where he started his legitimate business enterprises, and Las Vegas was where he enjoyed legitimacy once again, though in a state where everything wrong in Cleveland was right again.

In Cleveland, Dalitz maintained such a low profile that few residents knew he was the most important Jewish organized criminal in the nation. He was an innovator in creating a business model for murder, a man who developed the entertainment concepts that would later help speed the development of Las Vegas and the role model/mentor for Meyer Lansky. Dalitz technically deserves his own book, but that is not possible here. Instead, let us look at portions of the life of the most unlikely bad guy to die of natural causes after a rich, full life.

Lou Rothkopf refused to testify before the Senate on March 27, 1951. He was arrested for contempt. *Courtesy Cleveland State University Cleveland Press Collection.*

There never was a single immigrant source of organized crime in the United States. Most people would argue that it was the Italian American "mafia," which resulted from large numbers of southern Italians immigrating at the end of the nineteenth century. Instead, there were three separate groups responding in somewhat similar ways to the lives they had led under the abusive Catholic Church and civil leaders, the latter including invaders from northern Italy, the Arab world, the Spanish and the Normans of France.

Some Cleveland mob historians tend to think of the Italian Mafia as Sicilian, and some members were. However, emigrants from Naples brought with them the Comorra, and emigrants from Calabria had the Calabrian Mafia. They were independent of one another, a fact obvious in the early meaning of the term mafia, focusing on strength of character and close family life. Only among the immigrants at the end of the nineteenth century had the term been co-opted and corrupted by criminals and vigilantes whose focus was on vengeance, violence and killing as the first choice for achieving

Moe Dalitz at the Kefauver hearings in 1951. *Courtesy Cleveland State University Cleveland Press Collection.*

one's end. The elaborate ceremonies (See Angelo Lonardo's becoming a made man at the Statler Hotel) and so-called code of honor more often than not masked a self-centered brutality.

It is better to talk about organized crime when detailing Cleveland mob activity than it is to use the word mafia. Low-income immigrants moving into a new city in a new country where the language, the food and the social customs were all unfamiliar tended to live in neighborhoods with immigrants from similar areas. The Irish stayed with other Irish. A place Clevelanders called "Little Italy" might actually be home almost exclusively to Sicilians, Milanese or Calabrians. Jews, many from Russia and others from Eastern Europe, settled with other Jews, and so on. If there was more than one such neighborhood, the difference was usually the education and income of the first-generation residents. However they came, wherever they lived, the children turned to either education or street crime in the neighborhoods where they were raised (high school diplomas were relatively rare and thus a high school education was respected). Among such graduates were youth who went on to professions such as medicine and law, though the latter often involved getting a job in a law office, reading law books, asking questions of the practicing attorney, and then taking the bar exam without ever setting foot in a college.)

Morris Barney Dalitz, a Jewish kid born in Boston on Christmas Eve in 1899, knew little or nothing of the Italian criminal world when first growing up. His father, Barney, a U.S. citizen for four years when his son was born, was a man he adored and from whom he tried to learn as much about business as possible.

Barney's interest was in running a laundry, and when the family relocated to Ann Arbor Michigan, Barney opened the Varsity Laundry just outside the University of Michigan. The income was steady and predictable. Graduating seniors moving away from the area were replaced by freshmen in need of the same services. Expansion meant service contracts for cleaning uniforms, linens and other items for restaurants, hotels and similar commercial establishments. The work assured a man could take care of his family, set aside money for the future and pass on a business that would provide a solid future for the next generation as well.

Moe worked with his father, as did his brother, Louis. Later, when Moe was investing in both legitimate and criminal enterprises, he would have his own laundries that he separated between those he considered family businesses, like Varsity, and those he bought with money from the Cleveland Syndicate he later founded. The former provided a legitimate source of income. The latter were run with the highest of standards, but during off hours the equipment was used, in part, for crime. As to the profits, they were as likely to be invested in an illegal enterprise as a legitimate one. The only concern was that his employees never give less than the finest possible service because to do so would be to disgrace his father's name.

(The Dalitz-owned laundries eventually included the Michigan Industrial Laundry Company, the Detroit Supply System and the Michigan Overall Cleaners. The latter two merged into a company he and his brother, Louis, named the Modern Overall Cleaners. Along the way he was given the nickname "the Chinaman" because so many Chinese immigrants opened laundries that the idea of laundries being run solely by Orientals had become a cliché. Dalitz also began using the last name Davis whenever he felt one of his disreputable activities might get his name in the paper and to use "Dalitz" would be to dishonor his father at such times.)

When Moe eventually began using Cleveland as his base, he found he could be most effective relying on the collective wisdom of three associates—Morris "the Banker" Kleinman, Louis Rothkopf and Sam Tucker. They, along with Moe Dalitz (aka Moe Davis) trusted each other implicitly in planning both legitimate and criminal enterprises. They became known as the Cleveland Syndicate, a group of men who would have been successful in any business they tried. Their legitimate holdings ranged from the Pioneer Linen Supply laundry and Liberty Ice Cream Company to Milco Sales, Berdine Realty, partial holdings in the Detroit Steel Company and Reliance Steel Company, Dalitz Realty and a portion of the Chicago & Rock Island Railroad. Disreputable operations would range from nightclubs offering illegal gambling and liquor to Molaska, the largest bootleg alcohol operation in the United States that was started at the end of Prohibition.

Dalitz first became involved with criminal activity when he was fifteen years old and moved from Ann Arbor to Detroit to live with relatives while attending Central High School. Although considered brilliant, he was more interested in the streets than in regularly attending classes. He failed four classes and dropped out of school before his junior year.

Moe began hanging out with a group of teens and young adults whose de facto leaders were the Bernstein brothers—Abe, who eventually was considered Detroit's first Jewish godfather, Isadore (Izzy), Joe and Raymond. They were not a gang so much as neighborhood kids with a taste for the fast life, easy money and a willingness to commit any crime that offered a quick payoff. Several of them were boxers who trained at Harry Harris's Fairview Club, a skill that was highly desired for extortion, hijackings and strong-arm theft.

It was the news media of the day that turned the loosely connected group of friends in the low-income area of Detroit's Jewish immigrant community of "Little Jerusalem" (Oakland Avenue) into the Purple Gang. At no time were there more than one hundred youths involved with Purple Gang crimes, and the area where they operated had a Jewish population of approximately thirty-five thousand, the vast majority hardworking and encouraging their sons to seek a better life than they had known.

The young men considered part of the Purple Gang benefited from Prohibition as they became "muscle" for or against bootleggers in the

Interior of part of the Mounds Club. July 10, 1950. *Courtesy Cleveland State University Cleveland Press Collection.*

region. Sometimes they would hijack truckloads and boatloads of whiskey, selling it to clubs and restaurants, rival bootleggers or even law enforcement. Sometimes they would reverse the action, serving as guards for alcohol being transported. They worked for whoever paid them, sometimes acting as guards one time and robbers the next, with the alcohol being transported by the same bootleggers each instance. Those who stayed out of jail matured and became more professional at a time criminal opportunities seemed greater than at any previous period in their lives.

Moe Dalitz, for example, opened his first Detroit laundry in 1920, just before Prohibition became the law of the land. That same period, the city had 1,500 saloons, clubs and other establishments that sold liquor—a number about average for larger cities throughout the country. Five years later, there were 15,000 illegal saloons in Detroit; the entertainment culture of the city, like the culture of the nation, having changed. Previously, many people enjoyed an occasional drink after work or with a meal. A defiant populous greeted Prohibition by turning going out for drinks a form of entertainment in itself.

Bingo at the Thomas Club on August 13, 1946. As would become the practice in Las Vegas, the clubs Dalitz and his associates developed always offered as many family—or at least adult—options as possible. *Courtesy Cleveland State University Cleveland Press Collection.*

Moe Dalitz's activities during this period are not well-known other than the certainty that he placed the operation of the laundry ahead of the criminal activities, a different situation from his brother and laundry business partner, Louis, who was convicted of illegal liquor activities in 1922. The fine was just one hundred dollars and there was no jail time.

In 1925, Moe Dalitz found himself and his friends in the Purple Gang on both sides of what was known as the Cleaners and Dyers War. This was a simple conflict that quickly grew extremely violent.

The Union of Dyers and Cleaners in Detroit was meant to involve everyone in the business, including the Dalitz brothers. The average person on the street knew that all laundries were essentially the same. You took your clothes to whichever laundry was close, certain that the price would be consistent with others in surrounding neighborhoods. If one laundry charged more than another, you went elsewhere, and this was the problem. The union president, Sam Polakoff, and one of the members, Sam Sigman, wanted to raise their prices. Expenses were not up, and steady profit was being made—they just wanted more money. But unless they could convince the region's laundry owners to raise their prices, an increase would cost them business and would not enhance their profits. Everyone had to act in concert as Polakoff and Sigman explained to their members.

The arguments for and against the changes gradually became entrenched in the minds of the members. Reason was not effective anymore for both sides. Soon the organization leaders and some of the members replaced reasoned arguments with violence, occasionally enlisting members of the Purple Gang to handle beatings, killings and the destruction of businesses with uncooperative owners.

The violence became known as the Cleaners and Dyers War, and it involved members of the Purple Gang, dissident cleaners and others. It lasted more than two years before someone decided to stop the problem at its source. Polakoff and Sigman were murdered, and although several of the gang members involved in the war were indicted, all were acquitted.

There is little known about whether the Dalitz brothers were actively involved with the conflict, but it was not long afterward that Moe developed ways to more effectively utilize the equipment used by his laundries. It was an approach that convinced him to relocate to Ohio where he could take advantage of the proximity to Canada.

DALITZ BROADENS HIS ACTIVITIES AND FORMS THE CLEVELAND SYNDICATE

Moe Dalitz found the same types of youths in Cleveland that he had known when working with the Purple Gang in Detroit. These were also tough-guy immigrant kids who found Cleveland a mecca for the foreign born. Some of the youths were Italian, others Central and Eastern European Jews. By the 1920s, when Moe was juggling activities at his laundry—with the Purple Gang—and dealing with the violence of the Cleaners and Dyers War, more than half the children in Ohio's public schools were learning English as a second language. Neighborhoods were being dominated by gangs of boys in much the manner Moe experienced in Detroit. And though the image of organized crime was Italian, Cleveland had the eighth-largest Jewish population of any city in the world, and a number of the young men involved themselves with bootlegging and related crimes.

Prosecutor Frank Cullitan examines a small cache of weapons and money (most of the coins are silver dollars) in the Thomas Club on January 13, 1936. The money was enough to support a family of four for many weeks, and it was just a portion of one night's take. *Courtesy Cleveland State University Cleveland Press Collection.*

Dalitz recognized that the divisiveness of ethnic gangs fighting for domination instead of working together for mutual benefit. He began making the connections needed to assure the various gangs were united in their actions instead of constantly being at war, constantly having to bury friends and neighbors.

On a personal basis Moe assembled a trusted group of friends—Morris Kleinman, Louis Rothkopf and Sam Tucker—who, with Dalitz, formed the Cleveland Syndicate. They shared investment money and financial risk and protected one another from criminal indictments whenever possible. These were men who would continue as friends and associates the rest of their lives. At the same time, they periodically supplemented their numbers with men they trusted for one deal or another, including Chuck Polizzi and the Irish Tommy McGinty. Ultimately, they worked with Italians, other Jews, Irish and Greek mobsters, all of them benefiting from not having to continue the violence that had killed so many in the recent past. They also utilized Moe's past friendships with members of the Purple Gang when they needed to import muscle or were investing in enterprises back in Michigan and needed a Detroit presence.

BLOODY BUSINESS

It would be simplistic to say that Moe Dalitz wanted to end all the violence often associated with organized crime in the 1930s. Instead, he was tired of thugs, of men who only understood maiming or killing others to settle their disputes. Murder, in Dalitz's thinking, was a tool of business, and businessmen did not alienate or destroy their customers. They worked behind the scenes to assure that their activities would run smoothly. Sometimes that meant supplying a bribe to a member of law enforcement, and other times it meant documenting a seemingly honest man's dirty little secrets, then making it clear that he act appropriately to keep the information from becoming public. And sometimes there was no alternative to the need to kill the person who had become an obstacle to their latest venture.

Typical of the problems for which Dalitz saw no alternative other than murder was the case of a former Cleveland city councilman who had been in the midst of the extensive political corruption that had been a fact of the city's life for more than two decades. He was facing legal problems and seemed likely to trade information for leniency in court. Any revelations he might make would bring trouble for the syndicate's operations as well as the corrupt politicians, and that could not be tolerated.

The former councilman, William Potter, had to die, and how this was accomplished was typical Dalitz.

CHAPTER 12
KILLING WILLIAM POTTER

They were just friends—Louis Rothkopf (aka Louis Rhode aka Louis Collins aka Rhody), Moe Davis (aka Moe Dalitz), when he wasn't being a bad boy, and Hymie "Pittsburgh Hymie" Martin. They were in the liquor business together, and Pittsburgh Hymie also liked to stop by the Prospect Advertising Company that was run by Davis and Maurice Kleinman. Nothing seemed particularly unusual when they got together in the late afternoon on February 3, 1931, not even when Rothkopf left the two of them alone. Finally, their business accomplished, Pittsburgh Hymie left his friend. The time was unknown but well before 5:00 p.m. when Mrs. Fred Laub, the janitress of the building, entered suite four of an apartment at 880 Parkwood Drive and started screaming.

Although Mrs. Laub did not know the building tenant, she was aware that L.M. Marcus of Philadelphia had rented suite four a few weeks earlier, on January 8. He said he was not moving in immediately but would be living there when his wife arrived from Philadelphia. He paid his rent and was not seen again.

Also on February 3, William Potter, formerly a Cleveland city councilman, told his wife that he had work to do much of the day. He left home at 9:00 a.m., and when he realized he was going to be later than expected, called her at 4:00 p.m. to tell her that he had additional business to attend to. He would be later than expected. His voice was calm—seemingly unconcerned about anything out of the ordinary. He would not be seen again until Mrs. Laub entered apartment four.

From the report of Cornelius Cody, chief inspector of detectives, Cleveland Police Department:

> *With Sergeant Hogan and Detective Buttner, I investigated the murder of William E. Potter, age 45 years, of 1842 Rudwick Road, who was found murdered in Suite 4, 880 Parkwood Drive, about 5 this P.M. by Mrs. Fred Laub, janitress of this apartment.*
>
> *We went to the scene of the crime and found the body slumped on the couch in the living room. The upper part of the body on the couch and the legs on the floor. The body was fully clothed and the hat under the body. The head and body were badly swollen and decomposed and had probably been there since Tuesday evening, February 3, 1931, at which time Potter was last seen alive.*
>
> *The body was conveyed to the County Morgue where a post was had which disclosed a bullet wound from the left to the right through the head just back of the ear. Bullet was found in the dried blood in the couch and is a 38 steel-nosed bullet. There was also a laceration on the left side of the head where a bullet had grazed the skin and passed through the hat and went into the side of the wall and was later recovered.*
>
> *In the pockets of the dead man was cash $1.78, watch, chain, and knife, and papers of no value.*

William E. Potter was a man of past importance and present notoriety. He had been in city politics as a councilman and close associate of Maurice Maschke, the head of the Republican political machine. He had also been involved in land scandals that led to him facing trial in 1929. There was no question of his guilt, and when he was acquitted, it was obvious to those who knew the various players in the case that he had been politically protected. The acquittal was a reward for past favors and a bribe to assure he would continue to keep his mouth shut.

The daily newspapers had long wanted to go after the corrupt Republican political machine and reveal the full history of Potter. His murder gave journalists the opportunity they had been seeking for several years. They could finally use the officially unsolved case as a way to put pressure on the corrupt politicians who dominated city government. Each day, each month and each year that passed was justification for exploring Potter's history, his connections and the reasons why some of Cleveland's most prominent citizens might have been involved with criminal activity Potter was planning to expose.

During the early days of the murder investigation, several facts became known. First, a blonde woman had apparently been in the "Marcus" apartment where Potter was killed. She was identified as Akron Mary—real name, Betty Gray.

According to the February 4 police report, quoted in Hank Messick's 1967 *The Silent Syndicate*:

> *There is a woman by the name of Fan McAffee in Akron, Ohio, who owns a high-class Speakeasy which is patronized by a high class of people, and the place, as well as herself, is well known by members of the Akron Police Department…* [The woman was supposed to be a] *friend of Akron Mary and smart. So is Akron Mary, who does not associate with every man that comes to the place; in fact, she is known as a high-class girl and she is well known by all the politicians.*

Pittsburgh Hymie, his name still unknown, was readily identified as the person presumed guilty of the Potter murder since he perfectly fit the description of the well-dressed man who had been seen by various witnesses in the apartment building. He was also presumed to be the man last seen with Moe Dalitz/Davis.

> *WANTED FOR MURDER—Make every effort to apprehend a white man, 30-32-5-9-145, slim build, dark compl., black eyes, long thin nose, looks like a Jew and said that he was Jewish, wearing blue fuzzy o'coat silk lined and looked expensive, was full length, black suit, long narrow, pointed black oxfords, light soft hat, was very well dressed. This man, who rented the murder apartment, can be identified. No. 2, a very attractive-looking blonde woman about 22 years of age, no further description, who was seen in apartment about day before murder. Wanted for murder of William E. Potter.*

Over time it became clear that Potter had to die because he was in some way going to expose the syndicate's Prospect Advertising Company, a major betting parlor and casino. Eventually the police widened their search, including not only Pittsburgh Hymie but also Moe Davis (as they listed him in their records) and Louis Rhode; the latter two were sought for questioning. It was presumed that they had disappeared into the east end of Cleveland's Jewish community where, to the bigoted police, all the men looked similar and their obvious hostility led locals to refuse to provide information. Ultimately "Davis" and "Rhode" were never found, though Pittsburgh Hymie was located and two decades later, on July 6, 1950, the rest of the story was revealed by Virgil Peterson in testimony before the U.S. Senate Special Committee to Investigate Organized Crime in Interstate Commerce, headed by Senator Estes Kefauver.

Peterson, then the acting director of the Chicago Crime Commission, related during his testimony that in the Potter case, Moe Dalitz got away with murder. As he explained, Pittsburgh Hymie was eventually caught in his namesake city. The first trial's conclusion was a foregone conclusion as witness after witness was adamant about what had been seen and heard the night of the Potter murder. There was no question that Pittsburgh Hymie was guilty. He was convicted and sentenced to life.

The witnesses had barely returned to their normal lives when they began to learn that telling the truth might be the right thing to do in a murder trial but it wasn't always the safest choice. They decided that maybe what they had seen on February 3 was different from what they had stated in court. The defense counsel requested and won a new trial during which testimonies changed and the jurors refused to vote for conviction. Hymie left a free man and returned to Pittsburgh where he became successful working in gambling casinos.

As Peterson summarized the long-ago case when appearing before the Kefauver Committee:

> On February 3, 1931, William E. Potter, a Cleveland city councilman, was slain in one of the most sensational crimes ever committed in Cleveland. The most logical suspect insofar as the murder was concerned was one "Pittsburgh Hymie" Martin. Moe Davis and Lou Rothkopf were with "Pittsburgh Hymie" until a few hours before the slaying. Davis was also with Hymie until an hour prior to the arrest of Hymie who was charged with the murder of Potter. "Pittsburgh Hymie" was tried for this murder and was convicted. He won a retrial, however, and was acquitted. It was alleged that Potter had been killed because it was feared he was about to expose some crooked deals. The police had traced checks written by a city official to the Prospect Advertising Co. operated by Moe Davis and Maurice Kleinman. In recent years Davis, Kleinman, and Rothkopf have been connected with the operation of the Mounds Club, the Pettibone Club, the Jungle Inn, located near Youngstown, Ohio, the Beverly Hills Club, and the Lookout House, near Cincinnati. It is known, of course, that Thomas Jefferson McGinty has been an important figure in the operation of the

Mounds Club. Several years ago it was alleged that Moe Davis was then connected with a gang which was known as the Mayfield Road gang. Some of Davis' former associates have included Joe Massei, of Detroit, Mich., Abner Zwillman, of Newark, and certain members of the Capone gang in Chicago. But Moe Dalitz, whose whereabouts were never a secret, quietly avoided arrest and prosecution for his almost certain involvement in the former Councilman's murder.

There was one other "minor" gambling problem in those early years of the syndicate's buying properties and quietly flexing its Cleveland muscle. On December 16, 1932, the Cleveland Syndicate officially joined with the Mayfield Road Mob in order to peacefully pursue business ventures. Dalitz, Tucker, Rothkopf and "Chuck" Polizzi represented the syndicate, though Polizzi was considered a stand-in for Morris Kleinman who had been sentenced to thirty-three months in prison for tax evasion. Polizzi would continue to be involved with syndicate investment and operations, but his share would not be the equal of the other three men. That would be given to Kleinman when he was released from prison. In the meantime, the men would develop what was officially called the Buckeye Enterprises Company.

CHAPTER 13

MURDER, INCORPORATED

Incidents like the murder of William Potter were necessary from time to time, and so long as honest citizens weren't caught in the midst of the violence, they improved the business climate for the syndicate. That was why Dalitz, along with Lucky Luciano, Meyer Lansky, Louis "Lepke" Buchalter, Joe Adonis and others established the organization called Murder, Incorporated. The business was primarily centered in New York, especially in the Brownsville section where a training headquarters was maintained. However, the concept, the structure and the business arrangements all had been personally reviewed and approved by Moe Dalitz.

The idea behind Murder, Incorporated was a simple one. A murder that is planned in advance, the type routinely committed by members of the mob, is one where the killer and the victim know one another. And in those unusual circumstances when killer and victim are strangers, they usually are connected through rival gangs or rival businesses where it does not take long for law enforcement to learn the relationship. That was why, except where the fix was in, most murderers were arrested and sent to jail.

Murder, Incorporated was designed to be a service business supplying professional killers in the same way that car rental agencies provided travelers with a vehicle to use when they were far from home. You want to kill the mob boss of Seattle? No problem. Murder, Incorporated would send a hit man who had never been west of New Jersey, never heard of the intended victim and had no connection with any people or organizations that might want the man dead. He would travel to Washington state, locate the victim, carefully note the man's schedule and find a time to murder him. He would make certain he was not seen, but even if there were witnesses, they did not matter. They had never seen the man before. They would never see him again. He left no indication of his identity, and there were no photographs taken. Even in the most unlikely scenario of a witness able to accurately describe the killer to a police sketch artist who flawlessly recreates his portrait, so what? Only the local and regional newspapers might be persuaded to run the image. Since the man was not from the area where he killed the victim, and since he immediately traveled back home, it would likely be impossible to locate the killer after he returned.

The men chosen to participate in Murder, Incorporated ranged from amoral men seeking a job where they would not likely be caught in the crossfire of a war between mob bosses to psychopaths who enjoyed killing but would limit themselves to victims for which they were paid. Each man was a proven killer skilled with one or more methods—knife, gun, garrote, ice pick through the ear and improvisational weapons. (One killer followed his victim into a movie theater, went behind him and smashed through his skull with a fire axe. The horror was so great that the theater patrons went running screaming from the movie, with the killer joining them in their race to "escape.")

There were several locations for Murder, Incorporated, though Cleveland was never one of them despite the involvement of Moe Dalitz. The primary training was in Brownsville, where a garage held a car in which the men could practice ramming an ice pick through a victim's ear and into his brain. There was a break room, refreshment area and all the amenities of a small college, albeit with fewer students—none of whom would you want to meet unexpectedly. However, no matter where a man trained or received his assignments, he was given a base salary high enough so he needed no other job. Each hit paid him an additional fee. He had insurance, medical care, retirement benefits and access to an attorney in the unlikely event of his arrest. The perquisites were equal to or better than what he would be paid in a traditional corporate structure. And given the fact that the Great Depression was still ravaging the national economy, there were few businesses paying as well.

CHAPTER 14

THE CLEVELAND SYNDICATE EXPANDS CASINO ACTIVITY UNDER MOE

The breadth and depth of Moe Dalitz's enterprises likely exceeded those of better known Jewish mobsters such as Meyer Lansky. He was seen as the first among equals in the Cleveland Syndicate, yet he made certain that there was never rancor among the four. All risks and all profits were shared equally. Even when Dalitz gained the national respect that enabled him to be a major factor in the structure and utilization of Murder, Incorporated, he acted as a simple, albeit extremely sophisticated businessman. And when he felt it was time to transition into the nightclub business, he never lost sight of the need to find even better ways to draw patrons. His constant fine-tuning of what his clubs would offer eventually led to him becoming a major figure in the development of Las Vegas. But in the 1930s, he was still concerned with the post-Prohibition world where he planned to both take control of existing successful gambling locations and create his own establishments.

The joint venture of the Cleveland Syndicate and the Mayfield Road Mob—the Buckeye Enterprises Company—made its first investment in the Harvard Club in Newburgh Heights, a Cleveland suburb. The Harvard Club was a floating operation located at 3111 Harvard Avenue when Dalitz and associates made their move. It offered every possible game, from poker to roulette to slot machines. There were bookmakers in the club, and the action—carefully controlled to work in favor of the house—was so extensive that the club became a desired destination for gamblers coming to the Cleveland area for business or recreation. More important, the games were

KENO EVERY NIGHT

$490 IN PRIZES

1ST GAME $50

NEXT 12 GAMES 20 EACH

14TH GAME 50

15TH GAME 150 EVERY TUE. $200

Keno begins 9:30 P. M. Come early

AMPLE PARKING SPACE

PLEASE BRING THIS CARD WITH YOU

OVER

An advertisement for the illegal Dunham Club. Notice that there is regular taxi service. All of the clubs were openly operating—proof of the vast law enforcement corruption at the time. *Courtesy Cleveland State University Cleveland Press Collection.*

arranged in such a way that they could be quickly broken down and removed through the back door.

Dealers at the Harvard Club as well as the plush Thomas Club, another syndicate-owned club just outside the city limits, had loaded dice and rigged roulette wheels for use as the dealers felt necessary. The Thomas Club's manager, Gameboy Miller, also kept a large quantity of quality counterfeit money for paying off anyone who seemed too lucky at the games. But it was the Harvard Club that was considered the most outrageous.

William Fergus was the first man to run the Harvard Club well before the syndicate became involved. Fergus was followed by the belligerent Frank Joiner and his more accommodating partner, Nathan Weisenberg. The Syndicate/Mayfield Road Mob wanted to own the Harvard Club, and Joiner was outraged that they would think he might sell. His opposition ended when he disappeared, only to be found upside down in a lime pit, his head and torso decomposing while his feet and ankles stood out like a

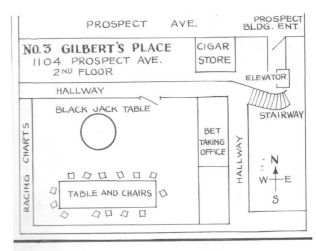

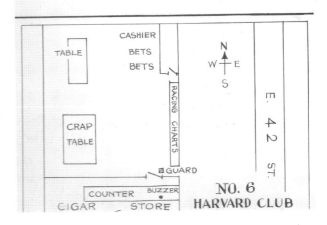

A sketch of the inside of the Harvard Club. The corruption was such that the press periodically made interior sketches and sent them to appropriate law enforcement as a way of prodding them to shut down the illegal operations. They were not successful. *Courtesy Cleveland State University Cleveland Press Collection.*

beacon to the passing teenager who spotted what was left of the man and called police.

The mob took control, and soon James "Shimmy" Patton was involved with the Harvard Club, as he had been with the race wire; so was Arthur H. Hebebrand; and always, quietly in the background, was Dalitz.

The gambling operation angered some observers and amused others. The Harvard Club, like the other gambling and entertainment joints, was a location that everyone either visited or knew it existed. This included some of the most prominent Clevelanders because, as Dalitz later joked to John Smith of the *Las Vegas Review Journal*: "How was I to know those gambling joints were illegal? There were so many judges and politicians in them, I figured they had to be all right."

The casinos were located within the jurisdiction of Sheriff John Sulzmann, mockingly known to reporters as "Honest John." He refused to investigate the gambling joints or to make a serious effort to close them down. Finally some of the reporters sent him drawings of the interior of the gambling casinos and added a map with directions to their location.

Sulzmann was outraged. He would shut the Harvard Club if he and a group of armed deputies arrived and found evidence of illegal activities. He alerted the press before leaving and then made the trip, a drive of a few minutes at most, in two hours. By then the incriminating items were gone, an easy action because everything could be stripped and removed while manager Shimmy Patton and others working for the club held off law enforcement.

The situation was so extreme that during one 1936 raid on the Harvard Club, Cleveland's new safety director, Elliott Ness, fresh from the Chicago battles against Al Capone, assisted as a civilian in an attempt to raid the gambling casino. Patton and others ordered Ness and some volunteers from area law enforcement to move away from the front door. He announced they would shoot anyone trying to force his way inside to shut down the gambling. While Ness and the others waited, the patrons, including Alvin Karpis wanted by the FBI for kidnapping, murder and other crimes, walked out the back, some carrying the gambling equipment with them.

It might be argued that the good guys won because the club was closed. However, as noted, this was a floating club. It could be moved and reopened whenever such action seemed necessary. Within a month, the Harvard Club had reopened in another building.

CHAPTER 15

MOLASKA: BOOTLEGGING'S GREATEST TRIUMPH *AFTER* PROHIBITION ENDED

W ell before Dalitz and the Cleveland Syndicate decided to develop nightclub/gambling/liquor establishments on a level of sophistication rarely, if ever, encountered in the United States, Moe determined that the end of Prohibition would mark an increased need for bootleg whiskey—not an end to the demand. This was because the government ended Prohibition but was still determined to reduce the sale and consumption of liquor. A series of legislative actions, combined with high taxation on legitimate distilleries, led to Dalitz and a series of associates—a who's who of organized crime—created Molaska on November 25, 1933. Assisting Dalitz, along with the Cleveland Syndicate, were Lucky Luciano, Frank Costello, Lepke Buchalter, Longie Zwillman and Moses Citron, filling in for his son-in-law, Meyer Lansky.

Lansky and Citron had an unusual relationship in that Meyer had known the Citrons since they were children. Anna Citron was long a friend of the young Meyer, eventually falling in love with him. He wasn't certain he shared her sentiments, and the 1930 marriage proved a strained one. However, she gave him the freedom to pursue his various enterprises without asking the wrong questions. He also became close to his father-in-law, Moses Citron, who gave his son-in-law a fifty-dollar-a-week, low-level executive job in his successful produce business.

Meyer took his work seriously, grateful to have a legitimate cover for his less-than-reputable activities. He increased the produce sales and generated even more money through the establishment of a series of Jewish companies such as Elaine Produce and Food Company, the Lansky Food Company and then Molaska. Citron chose to never question his son-in-law about the details of his enterprises, but he trusted the younger man's business judgment, not only working in Molaska management but also personally investing $120,000. It would have been a huge sum at any time but this was in the heart of the Depression when many Americans ate in soup kitchens and few had money in the bank much less money for investment.

Officially, Molaska was a company that processed dehydrated molasses for use in animal feed. The molasses was to be produced in Cuba, the arrangements made with Sergeant Fulgencio Batista, a man who rose to power in September 1933 and was personally paid millions of dollars by Meyer Lansky and the Cleveland Syndicate. Lansky, who made few mistakes in his long criminal career, was committing millions of dollars to the corrupt Cuban leadership with the thought that his future was running plush gambling casinos in Havana. The leadership was unstable enough that Moe Dalitz and the Cleveland Syndicate disagreed and eventually focused on Las Vegas as the place to spend the money they made in Cleveland. They did not anticipate the Cuban revolution that would bring Fidel Castro to power. Dalitz felt that the Cuban leadership was too unstable for any sort of long-term investment no matter what the past income had been. Lansky felt that so much money was being made from the Havana casinos, brothels and hotels that no one would dare stop the outside investment. He never realized that Castro was a moralist who felt that the Americans were exploiting the Cuban people and would shut down all holdings.

Molaska was established using seemingly honest businessmen to front for the criminals working behind the scenes. Moses Citron invested in Molaska to help his son-in-law, and he was officially listed as one of the many have been officially one of the founders; but it was his son-in-law, Meyer, who had taken over the Cuban gambling interests of the late Arnold Rothstein and was making made the shipment arrangements with Batista.

David and Sidney Kyman both had their names used in regards to Molaska. They were men who had long been in the produce business, one Lansky well understood, and toward that end, he had members of the Cleveland Syndicate approach them. Sidney Kyman was approached by Sam Tucker who wanted to use his name and not involve him in any other way. There would be no board meetings to attend, no money to be invested and no compensation of any type. He would simply be doing a favor, something to which he agreed.

David Kyman was only slightly more involved. In this case, the favor was done for Moe Davis. (Again, as much as possible, Moe used Davis for criminal activity in order to not disgrace the Dalitz name.) Kyman explained that he [Kyman] was never involved with the finances or management of Molaska, though he did attend two or three meetings that were held in Cleveland's Hollenden Hotel. He never asked questions and eventually told investigators that he had no idea if he had any connection with Molaska other than his name. He certainly neither provided funds nor received any money.

Considerably more involved was Ray Coal Company president Ray Tobien. Chuck Polizzi looked to Ray Coal as one of the legitimate investments being made and owned 25 percent of what was then a five-year-old business. Tobien loaned Polizzi what he estimated was around $5,000 to invest in Molaska. He received a stock certificate in return and then was told to endorse the certificate over to a New Yorker whose name, he thought, was Sapiro.

The name Tobien was unsure about was Moses Citron's attorney, Aaron Sapiro. Lansky's father-in-law gave Molaska $121,000 in additional working capital. A thousand shares of stock were then placed in trust with Sapiro. Moses had no meaningful involvement, working solely through his son-in-law.

Moe Dalitz's past and his involvement in the Cleaners and Dyers War suddenly came to the front of interconnected names that investigators were beginning to see in regard to Molaska. Aaron Sapiro was a Californian who was an expert on farming and knew the market for large quantities of dried molasses. His law practice represented forty-five farm organizations, and he was the go-to man for information about farm business concerns such as cooperative marketing. When he moved to New York, he rented an office at 500 Fifth Avenue that became the designated New York office for the Molaska Corporation.

There was another side to Sapiro. He had also experienced the Cleaners and Dyers War, though not in Detroit. The same problem existed in Chicago where Sapiro was the legal representative of the Chicago Laundry Owners Association. He also had been involved with Al Capone and others in the physical violence against the plants handling the cleaning and dyeing. In his favor, the attorney was acquitted in 1934 though questions remained since his freedom came only after the Illinois attorney general committed suicide.

At the same time, Tobien suddenly found himself treasurer of Molaska. He was not involved with actual management, financial planning or anything similar. He was simply given blank checks that he signed and then had them given to the man calling himself John Drew, president of the company.

John Drew, the president of Molaska, had only existed, at least by that name, for a few years. In 1923, when still known by his birth name of Jacob Stein, he had been involved as a Department of Justice investigator, ultimately testifying to the corruption of President Warren G. Harding's administration. One of Stein's most famous convictions was of another federal investigator, Gaston Means, who sold liquor permits for medicinal alcohol and other allegedly legal purposes (though not in the quantity he authorized) and engaged in influence peddling. Stein changed his name and used his knowledge of Prohibition-era activities to work for what he once might have considered the "other side": Moe Dalitz, Meyer Lansky, the Cleveland Syndicate and the others as they developed Molaska.

The various name changes noted in the years that marked the end of Prohibition and a new era of tax-avoidance bootlegging, gambling casinos and the like often had little to do with Dalitz and his friends trying to hide their activities. Instead, it had much to do with payoffs to law enforcement officers prior to 1933. Officers accepted quantities of money to avoid finding evidence of large-scale criminal activities such as the main distillery for Molaska. They did little investigating and made few attempts to build cases against anyone involved, in part because they often failed to identify the various players among the mob. The most ridiculous result came when they realized that one of the men they were seeking was not really named Moe Davis. Their "investigation" revealed that his "real" name was Fred Bennett.

Molaska worked from a number of business locations, moving operations whenever there seemed to be a threat from agents, largely corrupted, from Alcohol, Tobacco and Firearms. Ohio operations were to be the largest, and New Jersey operations were designed to serve the needs of the large population concentrations in both that state and New York.

The Cleveland distillery showed how massive and well planned Molaska had been. It was located at 5301 Sweeney Avenue, and anyone coming to the building would see immediately that it was empty—a massive, unused space resting atop a thick concrete base. The only curiosity was the fact that there were strong padlocks on the doors and a guard patrolling the property.

Large storage tanks were located nearby at Truscon and Fifty-fifth Streets and registered in the name of Molaska Products Company. Matters changed in 1933. Robert Bridges, a government investigator transferred from Detroit to work under new Safety director Elliot Ness, a man he held in contempt for having an ego far in excess of any past success in law enforcement, began identifying the full story of what was taking place with the Molaska Corporation.

A careful study of the empty building and the grounds both under it and all around revealed many secrets. The adjacent Sweeney Metal Company (5221 Sweeney Avenue) had a smokestack that was used by both the metal company and Molaska. The latter used large fans to feed the smoke generated in the distilling process into the neighboring smokestack so there would be neither sign nor smell of the underground plant.

A six-inch waterline had been carefully routed from the city system and was almost impossible to detect. Electricity could only be obtained legally, but the city records indicated that the Oxford Machine Company was using the electricity that was actually utilized by Moleska.

The system for transporting and storing the molasses was even more complex. First there was a storage tank located seven hundred feet away from the underground distillery. The seemingly isolated tank was connected to a sewer system still in place but no longer used to transport waste.

Near the underground distillery was a gas station that seemed closed when anyone went by. The building was unused, and the gas pumps seemed to be refilled every day by tanker trucks, except no gasoline was ever sold to the public. The truth was the opposite of what it seemed. The tanker trucks coming to the station were making pickups, pulling out two thousand gallons of alcohol a day instead of putting in gasoline.

There were also some external signs of a distillery that appeared as Cleveland's weather turned cold. Fumes from the alcohol combined with steam seeped through the walls and then stained the ice on the walls. It was a situation known to every investigator dealing with illicit alcohol being made in the cold winter conditions found in Chicago, Detroit, Cleveland, Pittsburgh, New York and similar regions.

The massive Cleveland operation was soon exceeded by one the syndicate ran in Zanesville on a location that allowed them to ship by railroad cars rather than trucks. It was discovered and raided by ATF agents in January of 1935. They reported that 5,000 gallons of 190-proof alcohol (95 percent) were being shipped in specially fitted railroad boxcars. Another 36,500 gallons of beer were also produced and shipped.

Molaska was so profitable that Dalitz, Lansky, the syndicate and their various partners decided to declare corporate bankruptcy and take a loss on their 1935 income tax. Then, after making additional profits through their successful legal manipulations, the company was reorganized and the stills moved to different cities. The entire fraud led to a government investigation, but almost no evidence was found that would allow for the indictment of any of the men involved. Instead, because of statements made on the telephone after a wiretap was in effect, Lou Rothkopf was sentenced to four years in the penitentiary. He served just eight months before his attorney was able to show that the wiretaps had been used illegally. Rothkopf may have been guilty but the case had to be dismissed.

> *The CHAIRMAN (Senator Estes Kefauver). Now, Mr. Dalitz…you fellows got your start by rum running, didn't you, back in the old prohibition days? Now, I am not going to go into any details, but Polizzi has told us about it, and others have told us about it. Now, is that the way you got your original money to make your original investments?*
>
> *Mr. DALITZ. Well, not all of these investments; no.*
>
> *The CHAIRMAN. I understand not all of them because some of them are very profitable. As a matter of fact, you have been making a great deal of money in recent years, so I suppose from your profits from one investment you would then go ahead and make another investment. Now, to get your investments started off you did get yourself a pretty good little nest egg out of ruin running, didn't you?*
>
> *Mr. DALITZ. Well, I didn't inherit any money, Senator…If you people wouldn't have drunk it, I wouldn't have bootlegged it.*

(From *Investigation of Organized Crime in Interstate Commerce*: Hearings before the Special Committee to Investigate Organized Crime in Interstate Commerce, U.S. Senate, 81st Cong., 2nd sess., and 82nd Congress, 1st sess., Part 10, Washington, DC: U.S. Government Printing Office, 1950.)

CHAPTER 16
CREATING THE PERFECT RUGJOINT (UPSCALE GAMBLING ENTERPRISE)

Senator Harry Truman had a different perspective about all the scandals of the 1930s. He was quoted as saying, "[Bankers] used no guns but they ruined the railway and got away with $70 million or more. Senators can see what 'pikers' Mr. [Jesse] James and his crowd were alongside some real artists." In other words, being a gangster might be in the eye of the beholder.

Moe Dalitz and his partners in the Cleveland Syndicate began expanding their operations. For example, there was the highly successful Beverly Hills Club in Southgate near Newport, Kentucky. This was an area popular with those seeking the type of sophisticated entertainment and gambling that would one day dominate parts of Nevada. It had opened in 1935 and was immediately successful for Pete Schmidt, the man who owned it.

The syndicate, aware of what Schmidt accomplished, decided to take control for themselves. They explained that they simply wanted to buy him out; it was something that would be profitable, at least for the moment, though he recognized that he wouldn't see any long-term benefits. He refused to sell.

The response was swift. The club was burned to the ground by a hoodlum named Edwin Garrison, who had been raised in Newport and was skilled enough to not get caught or to create a blaze the police could prove was arson. The one mistake he made was not realizing a child was inside the building. The child died, and Schmidt quietly sold out after the club was rebuilt in 1937.

George Angersola. August 6, 1951. *Courtesy Cleveland State University Cleveland Press Collection.*

The Beverly Hills Club, as operated by Dalitz and the Cleveland Syndicate, would one day be a model for how their clubs would fare when they moved to Las Vegas. Typically, a club might have a wire room to handle sports and related gambling. There would be casino-style games. And there might be some type of entertainment, whether some local musicians or a back room where men could take their "girlfriends" and "wives" for the night.

Moe looked at what was successful and began using the ideas in all the properties the syndicate built or purchased. First, the food was of a quality, quantity and price that made eating in the clubs a reason in itself for visiting them. Then he followed an idea that was similar to the attraction of burlesque houses using women who performed on a circuit—one or two weeks in Cleveland, then on to Detroit, Chicago, Atlanta, etc. Moe introduced the revolving chorus girls. Coming to a club on different nights would be a chance to be entertained by beautiful women you had not seen before.

(Note: Chorus girls in nightclubs are so much a part of American nightlife in cities such as Las Vegas that many people do not realize how innovative the idea actually was. There had been the perception that women would monopolize a man's time and energy. He could spend a little money and a lot of effort having sex with a professional employee of a club, or he could be guided into the gaming room where he might drop large sums of money. Dalitz and his partners realized that the greatest success would come from giving the clients as many reasons as possible to return to the clubs on a regular basis. It was better to have a man whose primary interest was the women than to have a man not go to the club because that was his only interest.

Professional entertainers—singers and dancers known from solo acts, the radio and the theater—were brought to the clubs, broadening the public appeal. Dalitz and the syndicate also hired young men to drive set routes in the community so a well-dressed couple going out for the evening could leave their car and ride in what amounted to a free taxi service. They learned to do anything that would increase the customer base, knowing that once inside almost everyone would spend more money than they originally planned. And it was this knowledge that would be taken to Las Vegas where Dalitz would create the most sophisticated casino of its day.)

The Kefauver Committee Uncovers the Past

It would be 1949 when circumstances led Moe Dalitz and the syndicate to relocate their operations to Las Vegas, Nevada. Two years later, after months of hearings in numerous cities and states, Senator Estes Kefauver and his U.S. Senate Special Committee to Investigate Organized Crime in Interstate Commerce, the Interim Report no. 3 was issued on May 1, 1951. For the first time, the story of the successful investments in gambling operations by Moe Dalitz and his Cleveland Syndicate was succinctly stated. The report revealed what law enforcement had either long denied or pretended to be helpless to combat, a partially true situation since so many were either incompetent or on the payroll of the mob.

According to the Cleveland portion of the report:

Organized crime in the Cleveland area presents the familiar pattern of a mob that had grown rich and powerful during prohibition days in the illicit liquor business and which transferred its activities after repeal to the even more lucrative field of gambling. The Cleveland gambling syndicate consists primarily of the following individuals: Morris Kleinman, Samuel "Gameboy" Miller, Moe Dalitz (alias Davis), Louis Rothkopf (alias Rhody and Zarumba), Samuel Tucker, and Thomas J. McGinty. Affiliated with the syndicate is an accountant, Alvin Giesey, who also functioned as secretary for certain corporations owned by the syndicate. The attorney for many of the operations of the syndicate is Samuel T. Haas. Haas was sought by the committee for questioning but has until recently evaded service of a subpena by going to Jamaica, British West Indies. This group has enjoyed close relationships and associations with certain gangsters and musclemen, who also participated in enterprises conducted by the gambling syndicate. Included in this latter group are the two Polizzis, Alfred and Albert ("Chuck"), John and George Angersola (alias King, James Licavoli, Jerry Milano, Joseph DiCarlo, and others.

The syndicate's major field of operations has been the conduct of gambling casinos at which all forms of gambling were provided from roulette to craps, from chuck-a-luck to horse bets and slot machines. However, in the many different communities in which the syndicate penetrated, it never had the monopoly that one has come to associate with syndicate operations. Thus, local mobs ran competing gambling enterprises. It should be noted, however, that in certain instances competing local enterprises were eventually absorbed by the syndicate; in other cases, arrangements were entered into by which the plusher enterprises were operated by the syndicate in conjunction with local partners, while the less expensively appointed places catering to the average citizens were run by local characters.

GAMBLERS MOVE TO ADJACENT COUNTIES

The story of the Cleveland Syndicate's gambling operations begins in the city of Cleveland. For many years, gambling casinos like the Harvard Club, the Ohio Villa and the Thomas Club ran wide open in the Cleveland. Governor Lausche, then a judge; Safety director Eliot Ness and Prosecutor F.T. Cullitan, acting in concert, closed these places in the early 1940s, and they stayed closed. Prior to this time, however, the Cleveland Syndicate had begun to expand into the counties outside of Cleveland. Apparently the heads of the Cleveland Syndicate knew that their days in the city were numbered, and they had previously decided upon various hedging operations that took them and their illicit businesses into the outlying counties of Geauga, Lake, Trumbull and Lawrence, where local sheriffs, prosecutors and other persons charged with law enforcement were more susceptible to gangland influences. The Pettibone Club in Geauga County, the Mounds Club in Lake County, the Jungle Inn in Trumbull County, the Colony Club and the Continental Club in Lawrence County and the Colonial Inn in Green County were among the most notorious establishments conducted by the Cleveland Syndicate. These gambling clubs operated in open defiance of the law. Transportation was arranged for out-of-town and out-of-state participants in the gambling games. Players were brought to these clubs from West Virginia, Michigan, Illinois, Indiana, Kentucky and other states. These gambling operations were finally shut down by the vigorous action of Governor Frank J. Lausche, who used powers available to him under the state liquor and fire laws to enforce compliance with the state's gambling statutes.

The Cleveland Syndicate, however, was resourceful and ever alert for opportunities to stay in business. Even prior to the shutdown of the various clubs in Ohio, plans were laid for an extension of syndicate operations into the wide-open communities of Campbell and Kenton Counties of northern Kentucky. Again the syndicate ran into local competition. In this area, the syndicate and the local talent operated gambling enterprises such as the Look-Out Club, the Beverly Hills Club, the Yorkshire Club, the Merchants Club, the Flamingo Club, the Latin Quarter and the Kentucky Club.

A MILLION-DOLLAR LOAN FOR DESERT INN

So rich did the Cleveland Syndicate become from its operations that when Wilbur Clark needed over a million dollars to complete the plush Desert Inn at Las Vegas, he applied to the syndicate and obtained the money in return for which the syndicate acquired over 59 percent of this gambling enterprise. In addition, syndicate members also obtained interests in some of the gambling casinos in the Miami area, such as the Island Club, in which Samuel "Gameboy" Miller was a principal partner.

In the Ohio–Kentucky communities, in which wide-open gambling had been carried out by the syndicate and by local hoodlums, officials were strangely afflicted with the inability to see the obvious, a disease which seemed to afflict law-enforcement officials in wide-open communities everywhere. The police chief of Newport, Kentucky, was probably the only adult in the city who did not know that there were wide-open gambling houses in his community. Any taxi driver could have taken him to them. The casinos were so unconcerned with the possibility of interference with their operations that they advertised openly in the Cincinnati papers. In addition, streamers advertising the attractions at these places were placed on the windshields of automobiles. It should be noted that the gambling rooms of the establishments run by the syndicate in Campbell and Kenton Counties, Kentucky, shut down just before the committee hearings in Cleveland on January 17, 1951. It is significant that an advertising card had been circulated, stating that the Beverly Hills Country Club in Southgate, Kentucky, one of the syndicate establishments, advertised that it would reopen on April 1, 1951, which, by a strange coincidence, was one day after the anticipated expiration of the committee.

The failure of law-enforcement officials to enforce the gambling laws was the primary reason for the existence of the gambling casinos in Campbell and Kenton Counties. The failure was not accidental nor was it due to the mere inefficiency of local law enforcement officials. As in other areas, the committee found a close financial and personal relationship between law enforcement officials and the gambling interests. For example, the sheriff of Lawrence County guaranteed the water and gas bills of the Continental Club, a notorious gambling casino that was run by a convicted killer. The sheriff of Lucas County explained his sudden acquisition of wealth by stating that he had won considerable money in betting, although he had never made such sums prior to attaining the sheriff's office. A proprietor of electrical appliance stores, who also ran gambling casinos, supplied the sheriff of Trumbull County with various electrical appliances, including an $850 television set.

THEN THERE WAS JIMMY HOFFA

Jimmy Hoffa had numerous Cleveland connections as he rose to power in the Teamsters Union. Bill Presser was the primary force in changing the Irish-dominated Teamsters into an organization run by men closely connected with both Italian and Jewish organized crime. Presser was a strong backer of Hoffa, and Bill's brother-in-law, Allen Friedman, helped set up the local union president with an underage prostitute. Bill quashed all indictments and publicity, gaining personal power that eventually placed him on the pension fund. And it was because of the size of the pension fund—approximately $4 billion when Presser was on it, according to Friedman's account—that Moe Dalitz was able to leave Cleveland for Las Vegas.

The Teamsters Union had always been less than honest in Cleveland, according to Allen Friedman, co-author of *Power and Greed: Inside the Teamsters Empire of Corruption*. Among other scams, the business agent might know that the workers wanted a twenty-cents-an-hour raise. However, the owner of the business either could not afford that much money for the workers or, more likely, did not want to pay that much. The business agent would meet privately with the owner, explaining that he could convince the members to settle for a fifteen-cents-an-hour increase over a three-year period, for example. Then he would tell the owner that making the arrangement would cost him a fee that might break down to a cent or two an hour for the members for the first year. The owner would pay the money to the union leadership without his employees knowing about the arrangement. Then the workers would be told that they would have to settle for the fifteen cents, but that was more than what they had been paid so that it was a victory. The fix was in, the workers were happy, the owner was happy and the leadership split the money.

Other scams were used, including two common ones when the pension fund loaned money for a construction project such as an apartment, a hotel, a casino or specialized business such as a party center. One way to steal was simple. The person borrowing made clear that he could afford a payback of $100,000 a year to be paid over twenty-five years, a hypothetical situation that illustrates the fraud. The payments made over that period of time would match the loan plus agreed upon interest.

Once the legitimate payment schedule was certain, the borrower would be asked to extend his payments for another five years, borrowing the extra accordingly. That extra amount, a half million dollars in this example, would be spread among the men running the pension fund. Since the borrower had budgeted for the twenty-five-year payback, adding another five years at the same amount was considered the price he paid for the loan. No one ever knew of the bribe, and in most cases the Teamsters Pension Fund loan was better in terms of dollar amount and/or interest than he could get from traditional resources. More important, the loans were given out regardless of the economy.

The second scam was also simple though more readily spotted. A man would come and borrow the money necessary to start or own a business. Again, here's an example: Suppose he borrowed $2 million for the project that was actually was worth $1.5 million. He would do the work, the business would be viable and he would make a few repayments. Then he would discover he could not continue. He had to default, and the Teamsters Union Pension Fund would take back the property as the borrower or his company went bankrupt.

After a reasonable time, the property would be put up for sale. The previous borrower would come and offer a sum of money that was much lower than the real value even when the payments he had made before the bankruptcy were factored in. The men on the pension fund board would sell the previous borrower the property for the offered price, secretly paying them a fee for their chicanery.

In Cleveland, this was a not unusual situation in the real estate field over the years. One twin building in downtown Cleveland was owned by a man with two corporations I will call A and B. Corporation A owned the buildings; Corporation B was a shell with no holdings. Both belonged to the same man. Corporation A defaulted on its loan and went bankrupt, with the owner arranging to auction the business. When the auction was held, Corporation B was the successful bidder at a price several hundred thousand dollars lower than the property was seemingly worth. The same owner possessed the property but the mortgage payments and total cost were much less than originally required. His scam did not involve any union funds, but it was typical of this type of real estate manipulation.

In the case of the 1949 Detroit laundry problem, Isaac Litwak was handling the negotiations between the union members and the laundry owners. This meant that Dalitz was being asked to talk with an underling, something he refused to do. Instead he insisted on working through matters with Jimmy Hoffa, the Detroit president and a former business agent who knew and had used all of the negotiating tricks in the past.

Hoffa was long considered the working man's hero for his toughness at the bargaining table. That was true to a point, but he was also a man who had no qualms about lining his own pockets. Moe asked Hoffa how much the Detroit president would need in order to intervene with the union rank-and-file and stop the strike. Hoffa was said to have replied without hesitation: $25,000. Then Hoffa, without talking with anyone else in leadership, made clear that the contract that would be signed would have no provision requiring a five-day work week. Everything else in the contract had long been acceptable to both owners and employees, but the continuation of the longer work week shocked those who did not understand how such matters could work.

Finally Las Vegas

Dalitz had long considered moving his gambling empire to where he could create the type of show business extravaganza: top entertainers—comedians, singers, dancer and musicians—with the finest food at reasonable to low prices, inexpensive hotel rooms and gambling twenty-four hours a day. He wanted a casino that was a fantasy, from having the slots with their bells, whistles and visual excitement near the hotel entrance to having no clocks or windows to assure the customers were unaware of the passage of time. He wanted beautiful women to entertain and others, seeming to be visiting tourists like themselves, who would stay by a winner's side, cheering him on, until he was just another loser. In fact, from the way Dalitz and others planned their locations, it seemed that the more money you lost, the better you were treated. The classic man who arrived in a Rolls-Royce and went home in a bus could do so in an atmosphere that seemed to assure he would have no regrets.

Dalitz did not design his own hotel/casino but took control of on what had been under construction before having to be abandoned for lack of money. This was the Desert Inn, the fourth major resort on the Las Vegas strip. It opened on April 24, 1950, arguably the most lavish property in the region and one that became "home" to major entertainers and high rollers.

As to the Teamster pension fund, the first time Dalitz worked with them was a decade after he and Jimmy Hoffa became friends. Instead of seeking Teamster money for another casino, Dalitz seems to have acted most frequently as a facilitator for other investors with their own valuable Las Vegas projects. His influence enabled the city to grow in ways that would have been impossible without the combination of mob money, Teamster funds and behind-the-scenes political influence that made Dalitz rich, respected and essentially untouchable by the federal government. The fact that he died with a personal net worth believed to be in excess of $100 million implies greater involvement, but he was so low key that for years the only car he drove was an aging yellow Volkswagen Beetle.

The 1959 Teamsters loan was for a union benefit, the Sunrise Hospital. Teamsters union employers paid to the hospital $6.50 per month for each union man or woman working for them. This was set aside in a fund that covered basic medical care as well as more advanced treatment when needed. The action was a unique humanitarian act in the city.

Moe Dalitz was involved with a number of casinos, a golf course and other projects. He helped assure Teamster money would pay for shopping malls and businesses that benefited both those connected with the tourist industry.

Las Vegas residents who knew Moe Dalitz would have either been shocked by the violence and other criminal actions that had taken place in Cleveland or they would have applauded Moe for using Cleveland as his proving grounds for new ideas for taking money from willing gamblers who will pay anything to be entertained. Whatever the case, his life in Las Vegas was one of supporting those who cared for others. The American Cancer Research Center and Hospital named him Humanitarian of the Year in 1976, and six years later he received the Torch of Liberty Award by the Anti-Defamation League of the B'nai B'rith. Seven years later, in 1989, Moe Dalitz shocked the underworld with his last amazing feat. He died of natural causes.

ABOUT THE AUTHOR

As the *Plain Dealer* put it in April 2009, "Ted Schwarz may be the most prolific author you've never heard of." Schwarz has been freelancing full time for nearly forty years. During that time, he's written well over one hundred books and more than three thousand articles and short stories for publications throughout the world. His books have been translated into more than a half-dozen languages, and several have been made into documentaries and/or television movies.

Praise for Ted Schwarz:

Kirkus Review on his biography of actor Peter Lawford: "Undeniably fascinating revelations…A gossip-lover's heaven!"

Publisher's Weekly called his biography of the stripper known as Candy Barr "[a] compelling, brutal tragedy set against a country's loss of innocence."

Axel Madsen, author of *Gloria and Joe: The Star-Crossed Love Affair of Gloria Swanson and Joe Kennedy*, said Schwarz's biography of Joe Kennedy "gives us a darker and truer picture of the founding father than the habitual spinmeisters and hagiographers."

Visit us at
www.historypress.net